SHORT BIKE RIDES™
IN OHIO

D1173241

Help Us Keep This Guide Up to Date

Every effort has been made by the author and editors to make this guide as accurate and useful as possible. However, many things can change after a guide is published—establishments close, phone numbers change, hiking trails are rerouted, facilities come under new management, etc.

We would love to hear from you concerning your experiences with this guide and how you feel it could be made better and be kept up to date. While we may not be able to respond to all comments and suggestions, we'll take them to heart, and we'll also make certain to share them with the author. Please send your comments and suggestions to the following address:

The Globe Pequot Press
Reader Response/Editorial Department
P.O. Box 480
Guilford, CT 06437

Or you may e-mail us at:

editorial@GlobePequot.com

Thanks for your input, and happy travels!

Short Bike Rides™ Series

Short Bike Rides™ in Ohio

By

Kay Wert Minardi

GUILFORD, CONNECTICUT

Cover photo: Chris Dubé
Cover design: Saralyn D'Amato-Twomey

Short Bike Rides is a trademark of The Globe Pequot Press

Library of Congress Cataloging-in-Publication Data
Minardi, Kay Wert.
 Short bike rides in Ohio / by Kay Wert Minardi. —1st ed.
     p.   cm. — (Short bike rides series)
 Includes bibliographical references (p.).
 ISBN 0-7627-0213-3
 1. Bicycle touring—Ohio—Guidebooks. 2. Ohio—Guidebooks. I. Title.
II. Series
GV1045.5.03M55   1998
917.7104'43—DC21   98-9767
                                                                        CIP

Manufactured in the United States of America
First Edition/Sixth Printing

In memory of Joan A. Minardi,
whose love was boundless.

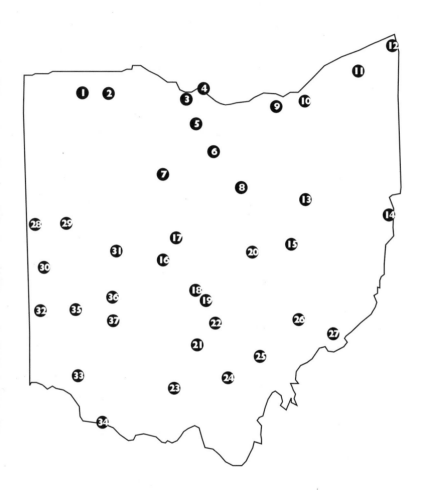

Contents

Introduction

Ohio is a mecca for cyclists. From table-top flat plains to steep hills, from deserted country lanes to the brick streets of restored nineteenth-century neighborhoods, Ohio has something for everyone.

At one time nearly three-quarters of Ohio's surface area was covered by ice sheets as much as a mile thick. These glaciers scoured out lakes and plains and left behind moraines, piles of debris from someplace else. Largely as a result of this glacial action, Ohio's terrain generally progresses from extremely flat in the northwest to extremely hilly in the southeast. Rides in the northwest are so flat, the only hills are the overpasses over the interstates. Rides in the southeast can be so hilly, a highway overpass would be a welcome break. Regardless of the general terrain, however, there is cycling easy enough for casual cyclists in every area of the Buckeye State.

Ohio emerged first as an agricultural power, so it is blessed with a fine network of farm-to-market roads. These roads have largely been abandoned by motorists for the interstate highways: Now they are perfect for cyclists who want to ride quiet country lanes. If you have limited your cycling to bike paths only, try a ride on these roads. You can find flat terrain, wider pavement and, in general, less traffic than on most bike paths.

Speaking of bike paths, Ohio is a leader in the Rails-to-Trails movement, with thirty-six trails totaling 294 miles and another fifty-two trails totaling a projected 613 miles. This puts Ohio in the top ten of states with rail-trails. If you have ridden only on roads, you are missing a real treat.

Finally there are eighty-one cycling clubs in the state, with more than 12,000 members. Join one. Not only will you find friends who love cycling as much as you do, but you will help support cycling interests so cycling continues to thrive and grow.

About the Rides

I have attempted to include rides from every part of Ohio in this collection. The rides range from about 6 to about 30 miles long, and most are within the capabilities of the casual weekend cyclist. Those interested in longer or more strenuous rides might consider combining several rides or expanding these rides to design longer excursions.

Most of these rides include one or more historic or natural sites. Over the years I have discovered that bike trips with a focus, some special place to visit, give me great pleasure. From previous experience and in researching this book, I found that Ohio has many historic and scenic sites. I hope you enjoy learning about Ohio's history as you ride these tours as much as I did while researching them. You'll find the "vital statistics" about select museums, parks, historic sites, wineries, and other attractions in For More Information at the end of the book.

Many of the historic sites included on these rides are maintained by the Ohio Historical Society. Admission is charged to most of them. If you are a history buff, consider joining the society to gain free admission to the more than sixty sites around the state. A full membership admits up to eight people for $45.00 a year ($40.00 for those 60 or over), while an individual can get membership privileges for $38.00 ($33.00 for those 60 or up). For more information, call (614) 297–2332 or (800) 686–1545 (toll free in Ohio).

Of course I also ride just for the joy of riding, and that "enjoyability factor" was a major component of the selection of these rides. If you're in that "zone" when riding is just too easy and fun, why not skip that Indian mound, museum or beach? It will be there waiting for you another day.

Most of the rides in this book are loops, for maximum scenery exposure. A few are out-and-back rides, usually because conditions are not safe or convenient to ride in a loop. Some rides combine transportation modes, again because of convenience or to add interest to your trip.

A number of these rides include state parks. If you need

more information about facilities at these parks, the state of Ohio has a toll-free phone number specifically for you: (800) AT–A–PARK. In addition, if you are interested in more general information about Ohio, call (800) BUCKEYE. The friendly folks at this number are happy to mail out packets chock-full of information and maps.

Each ride in this book includes a map; information on length, pedaling time, terrain, special sights and facilities; a general description of the ride; directions on how to get to the starting point; and a detailed cue sheet. The pedaling time was based on a pace of 10 m.p.h., but your time will depend on your own pace and how often you stop. Note that on the cue sheets and maps, Ohio state highways are designated OH. County roads are designated CR (county road) or CH (county highway), depending on that county's usage. Township roads are listed as TR (township road) or TH (township highway), according to local custom.

About the Maps

The maps are not necessarily drawn to scale. Some areas are enlarged to show more detail. Federal routes are indicated by a shield, and state highway numbers are circled County road numbers are boxed. Shorter route options are indicated by a broken line.

It was impossible to include every crossroad and landmark on these maps. Follow the cue sheets carefully. It also couldn't hurt to carry a photocopy of a county map. I have found De-Lorme's *Ohio Atlas and Gazetteer* to be a great supplement.

Time to Gear Up

What should you bring on a bike ride? Here are some suggestions, in order of importance (at least to this rider).

A bike. Any well kept, multi-speed bicycle should serve you well on these rides. The rides were chosen with touring bikes in mind and therefore keep to paved roads as much as possible. Note, though, that Ride 12, Bridges to the Past, includes long stretches of unpaved road. Although the ride is not impossible on a touring bike, it is more comfortably ridden on a hybrid or mountain bike.

A helmet. There is no piece of safety equipment that absorbs more bang for the buck. Cycling, though not necessarily a dangerous sport, does have its hazards. I know several people who have had serious accidents in which their helmets were split. Those people are back on their bikes precisely because they were wearing helmets. The cost of a helmet—whether monetary or in looking or feeling cool—sure beats the cost of brain surgery!

Water. When riding Ohio's beautiful country roads, you will notice water fountains are rare. On a cool spring day this can be an annoyance, but on a hot humid summer day when you are lost and fixing a flat it can be a much more serious matter. You can always stop and ask a farmer for a drink, but it is much easier to just bring some water with you. Two bottles for longer rides or very hot days is advisable.

Repair kit. Carrying a pump, spare tube, tire irons, and a patch kit turns a blowout into a fifteen-minute annoyance rather than an 8-mile walk back to town. Know how to change a tire before you go on that 25-mile ride to the middle of nowhere. Also take along a set of Allen wrenches, a small adjustable wrench, a small flat-bladed screwdriver, and a Phillips screwdriver, so you can make almost all other emergency repairs.

Lock. If you plan on stopping and being away from your bike for any length of time, it is wise to bring along a lock. Accomplished thieves can make off with your bike in seconds. Whether you use a chain, cable and padlock, or a U-lock, be sure to secure both wheels and the frame to an immovable object.

Bike shorts. The most common cyclist's complaint is "my bottom hurts!" Padded, form-fitting cycling shorts are a very effective remedy. The shorts are made to not move around when you pedal, so chafing is greatly reduced. They also wick moisture away from your skin to keep you more comfortable. If you are worried about your appearance in Lycra, bike shops sell cycling shorts that look like regular shorts but have a padded, form-fitting liner. For the ultimate in comfort, do not wear underwear under cycling shorts. The fewer seams there are between you and your saddle, the less chafing you will suffer.

Glasses. I wear contact lenses, and any time I ride, I wear nonprescription glasses, too. In the summer sunglasses protect my eyes from damaging and blinding sun rays, bugs, and debris tossed by car wheels or carried by the wind. They prevent drying of my eyes, too. In the winter I wear glasses with clear or amber lenses to protect my eyes from wind and debris.

Bags. A handlebar bag with a transparent waterproof map pocket on top allows you to glance down at your directions briefly while rolling or when stopped at an intersection. Photocopies of the maps and/or cue sheets in this book will fit in the map pocket, and you can slip the book itself inside the bag. You might also be able to fit a light, rolled-up jacket into the bag. Bags that fit on a rack over your rear wheel work well for packing rain gear and picnic lunches. They also are better than backpacks, which become uncomfortable and unsafe on long rides, because they raise your center of gravity. It is also wise to line bags with plastic bags if you expect wet weather.

Rearview mirror. This is a device you don't think you need until you get one. Mirrors, whether bike-, helmet- or glasses-mounted, allow you to glance at the road behind you without turning your head. This is especially valuable in heavy traffic, because looking over your shoulder often causes you to veer into traffic. Helmet- and glasses-mounted mirrors are more convenient than bike-mounted models, for you can aim them where you want to look with a small movement of your head. They also tend not to vibrate as much on rough surfaces. If you go to some of the larger bike gatherings in Ohio, look for Chuck Harris. He makes the sturdiest helmet mirrors I've ever seen out of spoke wire and odds and ends.

Gloves. On long rides, the extra padding cycling gloves give is a real plus. In extreme cases you can even damage the nerves in your hands if you ride too much without them. The added comfort of gloves is well worth the resulting funny tan lines. Plus they complete the fashion ensemble with your helmet and shorts.

Odometer. A bicycle computer is fun and practical. Not only can you keep track of how fast you're going, but you can stay on your route easier. The cue sheets in this book keep a running count of miles. Road signs and landmarks may change, but with an odometer and the cue sheet, you can be sure you are turning at the right place.

Jersey. Any comfortable T-shirt will do on a bike ride, but cycling-specific jerseys offer some definite advantages. First they are often made of specialized materials that wick moisture away from your body. This is a matter of comfort in summer and safety in the winter, because cotton remains wet from sweat. That dampness next to your skin can be annoying when it's hot and humid; in cold weather, it can hasten the onset of hypothermia. In addition the rear-mounted pockets on jerseys are excellent for packing your wallet, keys, tissues, and bananas. The pockets' placement on your back means they won't catch the wind, and the weight of their contents won't cause your shirt to hang down in front and interfere with your pedaling. Finally the neck zipper in most jerseys allows you to customize your ventilation.

Things to Remember While Riding

Perform a brief safety check each time you begin a bike trip. Check your tire pressure, brakes, and cables. Some general rules are: your tires should be hard (you should be able to depress them only very slightly with your thumb); your brakes should grip firmly well before you've pulled the levers within an inch of the handlebar; and cables should be taut, with no kinks or frayed ends.

In Ohio, as in most states, bicycles are considered vehicles, and their riders are subject to the same laws as motor vehicle drivers. Ride defensively yet courteously, signaling your intentions. Stay as far to the right as feasible, and ride in single file when there is passing traffic.

Be visible. Wear brightly colored clothing during daylight hours, and have and use lights if you think you will be out into the twilight hours.

Always wear your helmet.

Always carry water and a small snack. Drink before you are thirsty, and eat before you are hungry. You definitely don't want to bonk, or deplete all your energy stores, 15 miles away from the closest town.

On-the-Road Hazards

Cycling is perceived by some people as a hazardous activity, but it doesn't have to be. If you pay attention to the following potential problems while you are enjoying the passing scenery, you will greatly reduce the chance of an unpleasant spill.

Railroad tracks. Tracks at an oblique angle to the road are among the most dangerous hazards you'll come across. Check to be sure there is no traffic behind, then maneuver yourself so your tires cross the tracks at a right angle. Slow down and lift your bottom off the saddle to reduce the shock of the bump. If there is too much traffic to swerve to the correct angle or the tracks are obviously too rough, get off your bike and walk across.

Dogs. Out in the country, encounters with loose territorial dogs are inevitable. Many riders sternly shout "No!" to an approaching dog and pick up their pace to outrun it. Most dogs won't chase you far, because they don't feel threatened once you're past their territory. If you're going uphill or faced by a particularly persistent dog, you may need to dismount and walk away; keep your bike between you and the dog. Some people carry an ammonia-water solution in a spray bottle or a commercial dog repellent such as Halt! while riding. A shot of the spray right in the face is enough to deter most dogs. That, however, requires balancing the bike while trying to aim the spray and letting the dogs get close; sometimes uncomfortably so.

Bad roads. On the untraveled back roads we cyclists like so much, the surface is often less than smooth. You'll contend with potholes, cracks, bumps, and patches, any of which can dump you in an instant. Stay alert to road conditions, especially when speeding downhill. Slow down on really rough stretches. Lift your bottom off the saddle to reduce the shock of bumps.

Debris. Gravel, broken glass, and other debris tends to collect on the side of the road. Avoiding them will help you avoid spills and flat tires.

Puddles. Standing water is deceptive. It can hide deep potholes or debris that can cause a nasty fall or a flat tire.

Leaves. Fall is an especially pleasurable time to ride, because Ohio's hardwood forests put on a beautiful show of color. Wet leaves, however, are particularly slick. Like puddles, leaves also can camouflage hidden hazards.

Storm-sewer grates. In urban areas, beware of grates at the side of the road that have slots paralleling your direction. Bike tires can very easily fall between these slots and bring an abrupt and painful end to your ride.

Parked cars. Especially in town, watch for drivers emerging from cars parallel-parked on the road. Stay 3 to 4 feet from the side of a line of parked cars to avoid being "doored."

Metal-grate bridges. These bridges are squirrelly to ride across at all times, but positively hazardous when wet. Walk across in rain or early in the morning when there may be dew on the bridge surface.

Covered bridges. Most of Ohio's covered bridges have a wooden surface that warrants a unique approach. Usually there is a bottom layer of boards perpendicular to the route. On top of these boards are planks running lengthwise across the bridge, one set on each side a car's width apart. Sometimes the gaps between these lengthwise planks become wide enough to catch a bike tire. When crossing a covered bridge, first check to be sure no cars are trying to pass you from behind or entering the bridge from the opposite direction. Then, walk your bike across the lengthwise planks or ride slowly across the perpendicular boards in the center. The latter method is bumpy but safer if you don't want to dismount.

Cycling Organizations in Ohio

The Ohio Bicycle Federation, an alliance of individuals and organizations interested in promoting the use of bicycles for recreation, transportation and other appropriate uses, is an advocacy organization that represents Ohio bicyclists at the state level. It has a quarterly newsletter, the *Ohio Bicycle Communicator,* and publishes the annual Ohio Bicycle Events Calendar, the only comprehensive statewide listing of cycling events. The OBF's Web site is at www.coil.com/~bt364.

The OBF also has a list of all the cycling clubs in the state and is happy to help cyclists find the club closest to them. Contact Jim Guilford at P.O. Box 45346, Cleveland, Ohio 44145–0346; (216) 281–9933; or editor@crankmail.com.

For more information about the OBF, contact Chuck Smith, 825 Olde Farm Court, Vandalia, Ohio 45377; (937) 890–6689; or chksmith@aol.com.

Your Comments are Welcome

If you would like to suggest a new ride for future editions of this book or have comments about any of these rides, please write to me at The Globe Pequot Press, P.O. Box 833, Old Saybrook, CT 06475, or e-mail me in care of editorial@globe-pequot.com. I would appreciate hearing from you.

Flat Farm Frolic

Number of miles:	24.1
Approximate pedaling time:	2.5 hours
Terrain:	Flat to gently rolling
Traffic:	Generally light, except on state and federal routes; can be heavy around Sauder Village on weekends and during festivals
Things to see:	Sauder Village, Goll Woods State Nature Preserve, and Ohio's flat farmland
Facilities:	Restaurants and stores in Archbold, Stryker, and at Sauder Village; camping at Sauder Village or at Harrison Lake State Park (about 8 miles northwest); the True Value Hardware store in Archbold sells bikes and may carry tires and tubes

Perhaps the first thing that strikes most visitors to northwestern Ohio is the virtually flat, nearly treeless expanse. When the first European settlers saw this area, it was much more forbidding.

When the last glacier receded from what is now Ohio thousands of years ago, it left the low-lying Maumee River valley as a giant mud hole. In this stagnant swamp grew a dense forest dominated by elm and ash but also including oak, birch, cottonwood, and poplar trees.

This swamp forest looked like a black haze on the horizon, so it was named the Great Black Swamp. And great it was: origi-

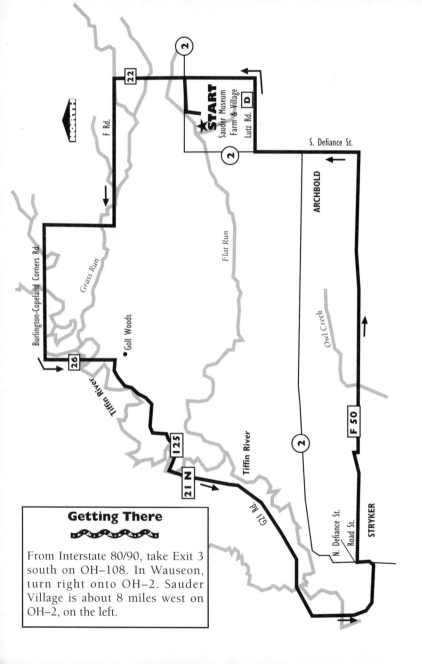

NORTH

② 22 F Rd. START Sauder Museum Farm & Village D Lutz Rd. ② S. Defiance St. ARCHBOLD

Burlington-Copeland Corners Rd. Grass Run • Goll Woods Flat Run Owl Creek

26 Tiffin River 125 21 N 621 Rd. Tiffin River ② F 50 STRYKER N. Defiance St. Road St.

Getting There

From Interstate 80/90, take Exit 3 south on OH–108. In Wauseon, turn right onto OH–2. Sauder Village is about 8 miles west on OH–2, on the left.

DIRECTIONS at a glance

0.0	Turn right from Sauder Village parking lot onto OH–2.
0.6	Turn left onto Fulton County Road 22.
1.6	Turn left onto CR F.
3.6	Turn right onto CR 24.
4.6	Turn left at stop sign onto CR G/Burlington–Copeland Corners Road.
6.5	Turn left onto CR 26.
7.5	Turn right at stop sign onto CR F.
8.0	Goll Woods Scenic Nature Preserve parking area is on right and hiking trail is on left.
8.7	Road becomes CR 27.
9.2	Turn right at stop sign at Y intersection onto Williams County 125.
9.5	Turn left at stop sign at T intersection onto CR 21N.
11.4	Turn right at Y to remain on CR 21N.
12.7	Turn left at stop sign at unmarked T intersection onto OH–191.
14.2	Turn left at red flasher onto OH–2/North Defiance Street.
14.4	Turn right onto Road Street.
15.2	Road changes name to CR F50/Short Settlement Road.
15.9	Jog right at stop sign CR 22.75, cautiously cross badly angled railroad tracks, then jog left to continue on CR F50.
19.0	Cross CR 24 at stop sign and continue on Township Highway BC.
20.0	In Archbold turn left at stop sign onto South Defiance Street/OH–66.
21.5	Turn right onto Lutz Road/CR D.
22.4	Turn left onto Clydes Way/CR 22.
23.5	Turn left at stop sign onto OH–2.
24.1	Turn left into Sauder Farm parking lot to end ride.

nally about 120 miles long and 40 miles wide, stretching from present-day Toledo south to Van Wert and more or less up the Ohio–Indiana state line. Although there were other patches of swamp forest left in Ohio by the glaciers, none was as large as the Great Black Swamp.

This mosquito-infested tangle of swampy vegetation hampered settlement and east-west movement across northern Ohio. Although Ohio became a state in 1803, it wasn't until 1834 that the first settlers moved into the Black Swamp region. It took these determined people from Switzerland and Alsace-Lorraine nearly ten years of working cooperatively to dig 100 miles of drainage ditches in the sticky mud.

After many years and much work, the land was made suitable for farming, and today it provides some of the United States' most fertile farmland and flattest cycling. As you ride easily along the lightly traveled roads, notice the luxuriant green of the crops and the neat farms.

You may encounter large farm machinery on this ride, and there is little shade on the route, with the exception of Goll Woods State Nature Preserve at Mile 8. This cool green tunnel of trees on gently undulating land near the Tiffin River is refreshing on a bright hot day. Use caution when crossing the badly angled railroad tracks at Mile 15.9.

Although you cannot experience the Great Black Swamp today, you can get an idea of the tools and skills needed to conquer it more than a century ago at the start/end point of this ride.

In 1976 Erie Sauder, the retired founder of Sauder Woodworking, established the Sauder Farm and Craft Village in Archbold to honor the memories of the hardy people who conquered the Great Black Swamp. Today craftsmen and costumed guides work in a complex of more than thirty buildings, demonstrating the nineteenth-century rural lifestyle. Various special events also are scheduled that focus on skills such as canning, rug-hooking, apple butter-making, and woodcarving. The village is open daily from mid-April to late October. Hours are 10:00 A.M. to 5:00 P.M. Mondays through Saturdays, 1:00 to 5:00 P.M. Sundays.

4

Wood County Wander

Number of miles:	23.6
Pedaling time:	2.5 hours
Terrain:	Mostly flat
Traffic:	Generally light, except on state and federal routes; can be heavy around Grand Rapids on weekends and during special events
Things to see:	Grand Rapids, Maumee River, Providence Dam Metropark
Facilities:	Water, restrooms, and sheltered picnic facilities at Mary Jane Thurston State Park; water and restrooms at Otsego Park; restaurants and stores in Weston, Tontogany, and Grand Rapids; primitive camping at Mary Jane Thurston State Park

As you gaze over the wooded banks of the Maumee River at Mary Jane Thurston State Park, it is hard to believe that during the heyday of the canals, the opposite bank was the site of a wild and crazy town.

On the north bank of the river was Lock No. 44 and the village of Providence. Soon after the lock's completion in 1839, Providence was known as the most dangerous stop on the Wabash & Erie Canal. This rowdy town had numerous taverns, and alcohol flowed freely, leading to constant fights among the canal crews. Conditions didn't get any better with the completion of the Miami & Erie Canal in 1843, when the Wabash &

Erie became part of a statewide canal network.

Cholera epidemics in 1848 and 1854, plus a massive fire that destroyed downtown in 1852, led to the demise of Providence and the growth in importance of the village of Gilead, across the river. Gilead adopted the more-sophisticated name Grand Rapids in 1868. A decade later, the railroad arrived and Grand Rapids became a commercial hub for the surrounding area.

Today Grand Rapids remains a hub for tourists visiting the restored canal and mill at Providence Metropark, shopping for antiques or specialty gifts, and for partaking in watersports on the Maumee.

This ride, which is mostly in Wood County, takes in the nearly flat farmland as well as the historic Maumee River. Your ride begins with an immediate foray into the countryside south of the river. A few creek crossings add some roll to the terrain and the villages of Weston and Tontogany, about 6.5 and 15.5 miles into the ride, punctuate your wanderings.

You'll return to the banks of the Maumee when you turn onto West River Road/OH–65, which will be your busiest road on the ride. Take time to appreciate the flora and fauna along the river, especially at Otsego Park (Mile 19.6), where there is a bird-watching room that is open from 10:00 A.M. to 4:00 P.M. weekends. You might even catch a glimpse of the bald eagles that nest along the river.

It is well worth the time to cross the Maumee at Grand Rapids to see Providence Metropark. The Metroparks Toledo Area have restored Lock No. 44, 1.5 miles of the canal and towpath and a canal boat, and tourists can hike the towpath or take a 4 m.p.h. "cruise" in the canal boat. Also in the park is the Isaac Ludwig Mill, which was built in 1846 and is the only remaining working mill operating along Ohio's canals.

To go to Providence Metropark, turn right to cross the river on Ohio 578 when you reach Grand Rapids. To avoid riding on busy U.S. Highway 24, turn just before the end of the bridge onto private driveways to the Isaac Ludwig Mill (left) and canal boat ride (right). You'll leave the park the same way.

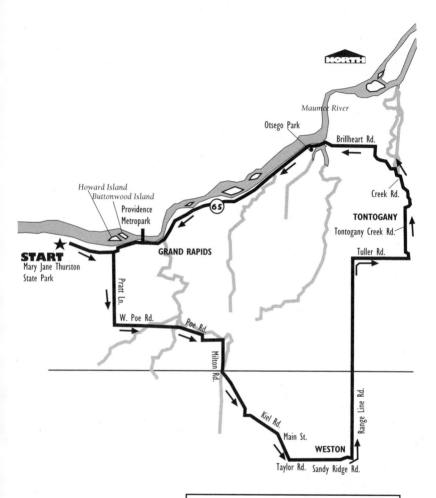

Maumee River

NORTH

Otsego Park

Brillheart Rd.

Creek Rd.

Howard Island
Buttonwood Island

Providence
Metropark

65

TONTOGANY

Tontogany Creek Rd.

GRAND RAPIDS

START
Mary Jane Thurston
State Park

Tuller Rd.

Pratt Ln.

W. Poe Rd.

Poe Rd.

Milton Rd.

Range Line Rd.

Kiel Rd.

Main St.

WESTON

Taylor Rd. Sandy Ridge Rd.

Getting There

From Interstate 75, take U.S. Highway 6 west. Turn right onto Wapakoneta Road. In Grand Rapids, turn left onto OH–65/Second Street. Shortly after town, turn right into the Mary Jane Thurston State Park Dam Area.

DIREC- TIONS at a glance

0.0   Head out driveway of Mary Jane Thurston State Park Dam Area.

0.1   Turn left on Second Street/OH–65.

0.2   Turn right on Pratt Lane.

1.9   Turn left at stop sign at T intersection onto West Poe Road.

3.4   Turn left to remain on West Poe Road (don't go straight on Custar Road).

4.5   Turn right at stop sign onto Milton Road.

5.3   Turn left onto Kiel Road.

6.4   At stop sign at T intersection, jog left, then right, to continue on Kiel Road (in Weston, the road name changes to Main Street).

7.7   Cross railroad tracks.

7.9   Turn left at stop sign at T intersection on Taylor Road.

8.3   Road becomes Sand Ridge Road after stop sign.

9.4   Turn left onto Range Line Road.

12.0   Cross rough railroad tracks.

13.8   Turn right onto Tuller Road.

14.8   Cross very rough railroad tracks.

15.5   Cross more rough railroad tracks.

15.6   Cross Kellogg Road at stop sign; road becomes Tontogany Creek Road. Downtown Tontogany is to right.

17.1   Turn left onto Cross Creek Road.

18.0   Turn left on Brillheart Road.

19.2   Turn left at stop sign at T intersection onto West River Road/OH–65.

19.6   Otsego Park is on the right.

22.3   To visit Providence Metropark, turn right onto OH–578, cross bridge over Maumee River.

22.4   Turn left to visit Isaac Ludwig Mill or right for the canal just before the end of the bridge.

22.4   To leave the park, return to bridge and cross river to Grand Rapids.

22.5   Turn right onto OH–65.

22.6 Cross railroad tracks and continue straight onto Front Street where OH–65 turns left.

23.1 Front Street turns left.

23.2 At stop sign, turn right onto West Second Street/OH–65.

23.5 Turn right into Mary Jane Thurston State Park Dam Area.

23.6 End ride by shelter house.

After recrossing the Maumee, you'll have a hard time resisting the ice cream parlor and other restaurants in Grand Rapids before rolling back into Mary Jane Thurston State Park. This could be the most difficult mile of the entire ride!

Erie Island Hopper

Number of miles:	16.6 miles
Approximate pedaling time:	2.5 hours
Terrain:	Mostly flat
Traffic:	Heavy tourist traffic from mid-June through Labor Day
Things to see:	Lake Erie, Kelleys Island, Glacial Grooves State Memorial, South Bass Island, Put-in-Bay, Perry's Victory and International Peace Memorial, Kelleys Island and South Bass Island state parks, wineries, and other lesser sights
Facilities:	Food, water, and restrooms on both islands; water, restrooms, picnic facilities, beaches, and camping at both state parks; water, restrooms, and bike racks at Perry's Monument

A short blast of a ferry horn will signal the start of your visit to two of Ohio's fifteen Lake Erie islands. A mixture of natural and commercial attractions awaits you on Kelleys Island, the largest of the American islands, and on South Bass Island, perhaps the liveliest of the islands. Schedule a long full day to enjoy this two-island tour, or—better yet—make your trip an overnighter by staying at one of the many island bed-and-breakfast inns, motels, or state parks. You don't even need your own bike to take this trip, because both islands have many bike-rental shops at dockside.

Your trip begins on the ferry docks in Port Clinton on the

mainland. If you're bringing your bike, you'll need to book passage on the Island Hopper ferry. Be sure to request the two-island package. There is a small bike fee in addition to your personal fare. To maximize your time on both islands, take the first ferry, which leaves at 9:00 A.M. Those traveling without bikes have the option of speeding to South Bass Island on the Jet Express catamaran and then traveling to and from Kelleys Island on Island Hopper.

Almost immediately after you get off the ferry on Kelleys Island, you can stop to look at pictographs on Inscription Rock on the waterfront at the intersection of Lake Shore Drive and Addison Road. These markings, which the elements have nearly wiped out, are believed to have been incised by Erie Indians about 300 years ago. The most impressive natural sight on Kelleys Island—other than Lake Erie, of course—is the 400-foot glacial grooves at Mile 7. These remnants of much larger grooves were scoured out of the limestone by the one-mile-thick Wisconsin Glacier about 25,000 years ago.

Leave the ferry at South Bass Island in downtown Put-in-Bay. Every weekend is party time at the bars and restaurants in this village on the waterfront. Minutes away, though, the atmosphere is quite different. You can ride down quiet roads flanked on both sides by woods interspersed with vacation houses and catch frequent glimpses of the blue lake beyond.

Just a mile from the marina, you can visit the Ohio State University Research Laboratory's fish hatchery. At Mile 13.2, you can take a refreshing dip at South Bass Island State Park beach or ride through the campground to see the ruins of the Hotel Victory. This hotel opened in 1892 and was the largest hotel in the world. It burned down in 1919, but the foundations are still visible.

The one place you must visit is Perry's Victory and International Peace Memorial, at the very end of your ride. It is impossible to overlook, because it's a Doric column standing 352 feet tall. The column commemorates the victory of Commodore Oliver Hazard Perry over the British in the Battle of Lake Erie on September 10, 1813. The battle, which took place

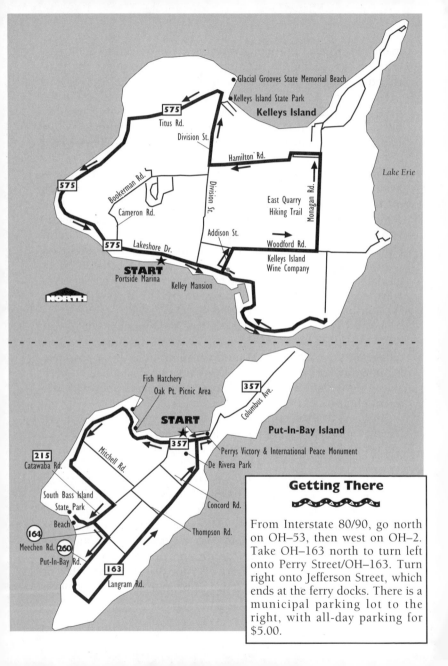

Glacial Grooves State Memorial Beach

Kelleys Island State Park

Kelleys Island

575

Titus Rd.

Division St.

Hamilton Rd.

Lake Erie

Bookerman Rd.

575

Division St.

East Quarry Hiking Trail

Monagan Rd.

Cameron Rd.

575

Addison St.

Lakeshore Dr.

Woodford Rd.

START
Portside Marina

Kelleys Island Wine Company

NORTH

Kelley Mansion

Fish Hatchery

Oak Pt. Picnic Area

357

Columbus Ave.

START

357

Put-In-Bay Island

Perrys Victory & International Peace Monument

Mitchell Rd.

De Rivera Park

215

Catawaba Rd.

Concord Rd.

South Bass Island State Park

Thompson Rd.

Beach

164

Meechen Rd. 260

Put-In-Bay Rd.

163

Langram Rd.

Getting There

From Interstate 80/90, go north on OH–53, then west on OH–2. Take OH–163 north to turn left onto Perry Street/OH–163. Turn right onto Jefferson Street, which ends at the ferry docks. There is a municipal parking lot to the right, with all-day parking for $5.00.

0.0 Turn right out of Portside Marina on Kelleys Island onto Lakeshore Drive.

0.3 Inscription Rock is on right at foot of Addison Street.

1.8 Turn around where paved surface ends and retrace your route along Lakeshore Drive.

3.3 Turn right onto Addison Street at Kelley Mansion.

3.5 Turn right at stop sign at T intersection onto Chappell Street, which soon becomes Woodford Road.

3.9 Kelleys Island Wine Company is on right.

4.3 Turn left onto Monagan Road.

4.7 East Quarry Hiking Trail is on left.

4.9 Cross airport runway at stop sign to continue on Monagan.

5.2 Turn left onto Hamilton Road.

6.3 Turn right at stop sign at T intersection onto Division Street.

6.9 Kelleys Island State Park Campground entrance is on right.

7.0 Glacial Grooves State Memorial entrance is to left. To leave the memorial and go to the state park beach, turn left onto Division Street and into the beach parking area. To leave the park and continue the tour, turn left out of state park onto Division Street.

7.0 Turn right onto Titus Road/OH–575.

10.4 Turn right at Portside Marina to end Kelleys Island portion of ride and catch the ferry to South Bass Island.

10.4 Turn right out of marina onto Bayview Avenue. De Rivera Park on the left has restrooms, water, and picnic tables.

10.9 Continue on Bayview as it curves around public docks.

11.1 Oak Point Picnic Area, with restrooms and water, is on right.

11.3 Turn right to visit Ohio State University Research Laboratory's fish hatchery.

11.4 Take very sharp left onto West Shore Boulevard.

12.8 Turn right at stop sign at T intersection on Catawba Road.

13.2 Turn right to go to South Bass Island State Park. To leave park turn left onto Catawba Road.

13.3 Turn right at stop sign onto Meechen Road.

13.5 Turn right onto Put-in-Bay Road.

14.3 Turn left at stop sign at T intersection on Langram Road.

16.0 Turn left at stop sign at T intersection on Toledo Avenue.

16.3 Turn right at stop sign at T intersection on Bayview Avenue.

16.4 Perry's Monument is on right. To leave monument turn left on Bayview Avenue.

16.6 Turn right at the Island Hopper terminal, just past the Dairy Queen, to end ride.

---

in waters just a few miles west of here, immortalized Perry, who afterward sent a note to General William Henry Harrison stating: "We have met the enemy, and they are ours." The victory eventually led to the establishment of the 4,000-mile unarmed border that we share with Canada.

Check out the visitors center at the base of the memorial; if you're lucky, you will be in time for a program given by a National Park Service ranger dressed in period costume. Also take the time to ride the elevator to the top of the monument and take in the marvelous view of Ohio and the now-peaceful waters of Ohio and Ontario.

Biking to the Beacon

Number of Miles:	18.5
Approximate pedaling time:	2 hours
Terrain:	Flat
Traffic:	Heavy from mid-June through Labor Day
Things to see:	Lake Erie, East Harbor State Park, Lakeside, Marblehead Lighthouse
Facilities:	Food, water, picnic facilities, and restrooms in Lakeside; water, restrooms, picnic shelters, beach (snack bar in summer), and camping at East Harbor State Park; many craft shops and restaurants dot this tour—don't pass up Toft's ice cream!

The Marblehead Peninsula, with its great access to Lake Erie and its islands, is a beacon to thousands of vacationers every year. As a cyclist, you, too, can follow the light to Ohio's North Coast.

If you don't care to join the peak traffic of midsummer, try the shoulder seasons. May through mid-June and Labor Day through mid-October offer plenty of sunny, pleasant days to take this easy spin across the perfectly flat topography.

A note of caution: Be extremely careful when turning left on OH–163 from OH–269 as you begin your ride; the traffic is heavy and fast-moving. Ride the paved shoulder on OH–163 as well as on any of the other busy roads on this ride.

You'll see a couple of historic markers on the right along Bayshore Road. One, at Mile 7.6, describes Ohio's first battle in the War of 1812. The other, at Mile 8.1, describes Johnson's Island, a Civil War camp for Confederate officers. Unfortunately the causeway to the island, just a couple tenths of a mile farther on, is off-limits to bikes (though not to cars). You might want to drive back after your ride to visit the island's intriguing well-maintained cemetery "guarded" by a bronze Confederate soldier. There is a fee of $1.00 per car to cross the causeway.

The highlight of this tour is the Marblehead Lighthouse, at Mile 10.4. It is the second-oldest lighthouse on Lake Erie and the oldest continuously operating lighthouse on the Great Lakes. Built in 1822, it sits in a small parklike setting with a few picnic tables. If you can, schedule your ride for the second Saturday of a summer month, because tours of the lighthouse are offered from 9:00 A.M. to 3:00 P.M.

You'll enter one of the more interesting villages in northwestern Ohio at Mile 12.7. Lakeside is a Methodist-affiliated resort that offers religious, cultural, and entertainment programming. The third week in June through Labor Day is Lakeside's peak season, and you will need to request a free pass at the gate to ride through. These passes mandate that you not remain in the village for any appreciable length of time, but you can ride down the streets to admire the cute Victorian-style cottages, and you might also stop to enjoy the lakefront park or get an ice cream cone downtown. In the shoulder seasons, your ride through Lakeside should be unimpeded by time restrictions or slow-moving traffic.

On the remainder of your ride you will see various tourist accommodations and attractions interspersed with all-too-infrequent views of the water. The best choice of all on a hot summer day might be to hightail it over the last five miles back to East Harbor State Park for a refreshing swim in Lake Erie.

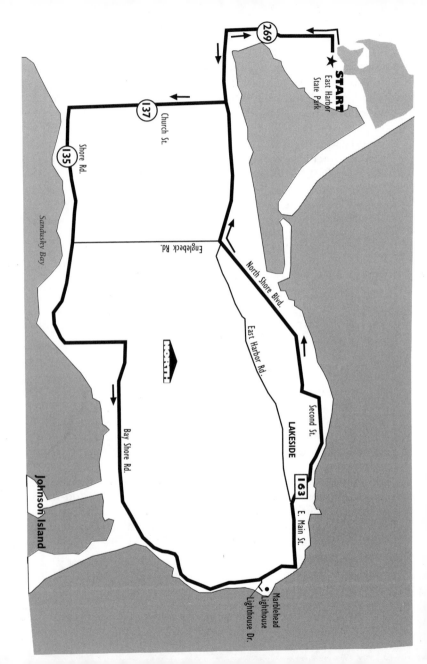

DIREC-TIONS at a glance

0.0	Turn right out of picnic area parking lot, then left at stop sign onto park's exit driveway.
0.1	Turn left at stop sign onto OH–269.
1.2	Turn left at stop sign onto OH–163.
1.9	Turn right onto Church Road/Ottawa County 137.

3.6 Turn left at stop sign at T intersection onto Bayshore Road/CR 135.

6.2 Dempsey Boat Launch area on right has pit toilets.

6.6 Turn right at Y intersection to continue on Bayshore.

9.5 Great view of Sandusky Bay.

10.2 Turn right onto Lighthouse Drive (see sign for the Marblehead Lighthouse).

10.4 Marblehead Lighthouse. To leave, go back down Lighthouse Drive.

10.5 Turn right at stop sign onto East Main Street/OH–163.

11.0 Good view of the lake and Kelleys Island.

11.7 Turn right onto Francis Street.

11.8 Turn left at stop sign onto Prairie Street.

12.0 Turn left at stop sign onto Stone Street.

12.2 Turn right at stop sign onto Elliot Street.

12.3 Elliot becomes Harsh Road.

12.7 East gate to Lakeside. Request a drive-through pass in summer months. Harsh Road becomes Second Street.

Getting There

From Interstate 80/90, go north on OH–4, then west on OH–2, then north on OH–269. Follow the signs to East Harbor State Park. Turn right at the park entrance, then left to the picnic area parking lot. Note that the picnic area's (pit) toilets are in a grove of trees up an asphalt-paved path to the right of the picnic shelter.

13.1 Park with restrooms and picnic area is on right.
13.2 Turn left onto Maple Street.
13.4 Turn right at stop sign onto Fifth Street.
13.5 Go out Lakeside's west gate.
13.5 Go straight at stop sign onto North Shore Boulevard.
15.2 Turn right at stop sign onto OH–163.
17.3 Turn right onto OH–269.
18.2 Turn right into East Harbor State Park.
18.4 Turn left to go to picnic area.
18.5 Turn right to enter picnic area parking lot and end ride.

Blazing Through the Firelands

Number of miles:	30.5 (22.3 for shorter loop)
Approximate pedaling time:	3 hours (2 hours on shorter ride)
Terrain:	Flat to rolling
Traffic:	Sparse, except in and around towns and on federal and state routes
Things to see:	Alpacas, Firelands Museum, stately homes, Thomas Edison's birthplace, Milan Historical Museum
Facilities:	Restaurants and stores in Monroeville, Norwalk, and Milan; bike shop in Norwalk

This ride takes you over beautiful scenic roads through flat to gently rolling countryside and the towns of Monroeville, Norwalk, and Milan (Milan is on the longer loop). It is an easy ride that will require far less than the "99 percent perspiration and 1 percent inspiration" that Milan native Thomas Edison said were the keys to his genius.

North-central Ohio got its start during the Revolutionary War, before any white settlers had arrived in the area. British raiders with the assistance of the infamous Benedict Arnold burned vast areas of Connecticut in 1779 and 1780. Those who had been burned out of their homes petitioned the Connecticut legislature for compensation, and in 1792 the legislature granted 500,000 acres in the Western Reserve, along the south shore of Lake Erie. The fire victims banded into an association and sent surveyors to lay out the land into townships, giving them familiar New England names. The settlers started moving to the

Firelands in 1809, laying out their new towns according to their custom: Thus we find attractive town greens presided over by New England-style churches in northern Ohio.

The beginning and end of this loop are very flat; farmers' fields are edged with lines of trees that serve as windbreaks. The most unusual livestock raised along this route are the alpacas at Mile 7.6, on Peru–Olena Road. Alpacas are South American mammals related to llamas whose wool is valued for making sweaters. These creatures are curious and will approach the fence if you stop to examine them more closely.

Ridge Road, at 8.4 miles, signals the start of a slightly more rolling segment of the ride. You will encounter several dips and rises as you cross and recross Cole Creek on your way to Norwalk. Traffic will also become heavier the closer you get to this city, which is the Huron County seat. Avoid the worst of this traffic by turning off Ridge on South Norwalk Road at Mile 12.3.

Norwalk has many stately one-hundred-year-old houses on Main Street. West Main Street from No. 39 to No. 200 was declared a historic area in 1974. Although the houses are not open to the public (with the exception of the Preston–Wickham Home, now the society's Firelands Museum), you may find it interesting to look at them from the outside.

The Firelands Museum is in the house you will pass at Mile 15.6. Newspaper publisher Samuel Preston built it in 1835 as a wedding present for his daughter. The rooms are decorated in the styles of the period, and exhibits include antique guns, Civil War items, pioneer and Indian artifacts, and various maps and treaties pertaining to the Firelands.

When you leave the Firelands Museum, you need to make a decision: Return to Main Street/OH–61 and continue on the long route, which goes through Milan, or continue downhill on Case Avenue and take the shortcut back to Monroeville? The terrain is mostly flat on both loops, but the longer route includes a visit to the village of Milan (pronounced *my-lan*). Expect a fair amount of traffic from Norwalk to Milan. Although this isn't the most direct (and busiest) route, it is only about 6

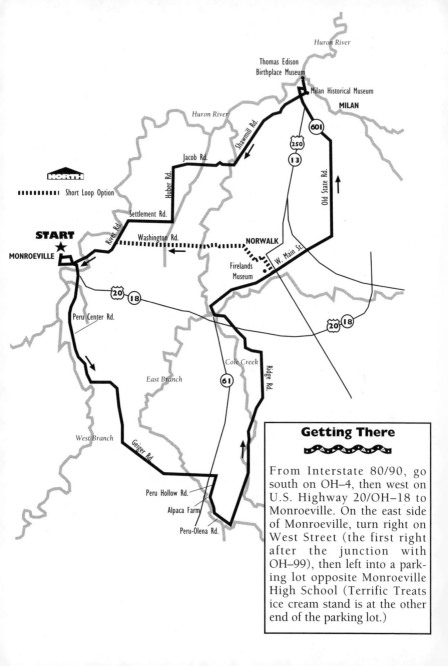

Huron River

Thomas Edison
Birthplace Museum

Milan Historical Museum

MILAN

601

250

13

Shawmill Rd.

Huron River

Jacob Rd.

Huber Rd.

Old State Rd.

NORTH

Short Loop Option

Settlement Rd.

River Rd.

Washington Rd.

NORWALK

W. Main St.

Firelands
Museum

START

MONROEVILLE

20 18

Peru Center Rd.

20 18

Cole Creek

East Branch

61

Ridge Rd.

West Branch

Geiger Rd.

Peru Hollow Rd.

Alpaca Farm

Peru-Olena Rd.

Getting There

From Interstate 80/90, go
south on OH–4, then west on
U.S. Highway 20/OH–18 to
Monroeville. On the east side
of Monroeville, turn right on
West Street (the first right
after the junction with
OH–99), then left into a parking lot opposite Monroeville
High School (Terrific Treats
ice cream stand is at the other
end of the parking lot.)

**DIREC-
TIONS
at a glance**

0.0	Turn left out of parking lot onto West Street.
0.2	Turn left at stop sign onto Broad Street.
0.2	Cross railroad tracks.
0.4	Turn right onto Brown Street.
0.5	Turn left at stop sign onto Monroe Street.

0.6 Turn right at traffic signal onto Main Street/U.S. Highway 20. Watch out for trucks.

0.8 Turn right onto Peru Center South.

0.9 Cross very uneven railroad tracks.

4.8 Turn left on Geiger Road.

7.2 Turn right at stop sign at T intersection onto Peru Hollow Road.

7.6 Turn left onto Peru–Olena Road (alpaca farm on right).

8.4 Turn left at stop sign onto Ridge Road.

12.3 Turn left at stop sign to continue on Ridge Road.

12.3 Turn left onto Norwalk Road.

13.9 Turn right at stop sign at T intersection on OH–61.

14.1 At stop sign turn right to continue on OH–61/West Main Street.

15.6 Turn left at traffic signal onto Case Avenue. Firelands Museum is house on right. When leaving museum, return to Main Street and turn left at the traffic signal. For abbreviated ride, skip to short loop directions below.

17.1 Cautiously turn left on Old State Road.

20.7 Turn left at stop sign onto OH–601.

21.9 Turn right at traffic signal onto Church Street and pass the town green.

22.0 Turn left onto North Edison Street.

22.2 Edison Birthplace Museum is on left, and just past the house is a plaque describing the old canal basin. To leave turn around and go back down Edison Street.

22.3 Turn right at stop sign onto Front Street.

22.4 Turn left at stop sign onto North Main Street.

22.6 Turn right at traffic signal onto Church Street/OH–113.

23.2 Go straight at stop sign, under former railroad overpass onto Shawmill Road. (*Caution:* 100 feet of gravel.)

24.8 Turn right onto Schaefer Road.

25.3 Turn left at stop sign onto Lovers Lane Road.

25.4 Turn right onto Jacob Road.

26.4 Turn left at stop sign at T intersection onto Huber Road.

27.6 Road takes ninety-degree turn to the right and becomes Webb Settlement Road.

28.6 Turn left at stop sign onto River Road.

29.8 At traffic signal, the road becomes Monroe Street.

30.2 Cross railroad tracks.

30.2 Turn right onto Prospect Street.

30.3 Turn right at stop sign onto Broad Street.

30.3 Turn left onto West Street.

30.5 Turn right into parking lot to end ride.

Short loop directions

15.6 To leave Firelands Museum, continue on Case Avenue away from Main Street. Follow Case as it takes a ninety-degree turn to right. Case becomes Monroe Street after the turn.

15.7 Turn left at stop sign onto Hester Street.

16.0 Turn left at stop sign onto League Street.

16.1 Turn right onto State Street at St. Mary's Church.

16.4 Turn left at stop sign at T intersection onto Washington Road.

19.5 Turn left at stop sign at T intersection onto River Road.

Now pick up rest of directions from Mile 28.6.

miles between these neighboring communities.

Milan is most famous for being the birthplace of master inventor Thomas Edison, but in its heyday this inland town was noted as a wheat port. The farmers of the area didn't have the network of roads that exist today, so the town fathers widened the Huron river for the 3 miles necessary to allow lake schooners to dock in Milan, 9 miles upriver from Lake Erie. The canal was finished on July 4, 1839, and Milan quickly became the world's second-leading wheat port, behind only Odessa, Russia. Unfortunately the advent of railroads ended Milan's golden age of shipping just ten years after it began.

On the heels of Milan's shipping boom, Thomas Alva Edison was born on February 11, 1847, in an unpretentious house at Mile 22.2 next to the canal basin. He grew up to become one of the world's great inventors, designing the incandescent and fluorescent light bulbs, phonograph, movie camera, movie projector, the alkaline storage battery, and more. Even today he holds more patents then any other American: 1,093. Today Edison's birthplace is a museum that offers guided tours to visitors January through November.

Just .1 mile down North Edison Street from the Edison Birthplace Museum, you'll pass the Milan Historical Museum. This museum, open April through October, invites visitors to wander through its seven-building complex to see how life was lived in days gone by.

Heading back out into the countryside, be careful at Mile 23.2 on Shawmill Road, where there is about 100 feet of gravel. Then as you turn onto Schaefer Road at Mile 24.8, be sure to check out the back yard on the right. It is a sight from days gone by, with antique cars and old signs decorating the place.

The two loops come together on River Road, at Mile 27.7 for the longer route and Mile 19.5 on the more direct route. From here it is about 3 easy miles back to your starting point in Monroeville.

A Ride Through the Muck

Number of miles:	24.1
Approximate pedaling time:	2.5 hours
Terrain:	Flat to gently rolling
Things to see:	Extensive vegetable farms in Ohio's "muck," vegetable-packing plant tour
Facilities:	Restaurants and stores in Willard and Plymouth; water, picnic tables, restrooms, bike racks, and swimming pool at Willard Park

No, this is not a mud-biker's dream ride; instead, it is a pleasant jaunt through a small region of Ohio with a unique soil that is excellent for growing vegetables.

"Muck" is a black nutrient-rich soil found in former wetlands around the appropriately named Celeryville. This soil is 35 percent to 65 percent organic matter, and it is excellent for growing celery, radishes, onions and various lettuces. Farmers here also grow cabbage, squash, pumpkins, sweet corn, broccoli, parsley, mustard, and various greens. The soil is so rich and the climate here mild enough that several crops can be grown each season. In fact, Buurma Farms' record for radishes from seed to harvest is eighteen days.

Begin your ride in the city park in Willard. You will quickly be in the country, on roads largely traffic free except for farm vehicles, until you reach Celeryville, about 6.5 miles into the ride.

If possible, turn left off OH–103 at Mile 8.0 to visit the Buurma Farms plant. Free tours are offered from 8:00 A.M. to 5:00 P.M. Mondays through Fridays and 8:00 A.M. to noon on

Saturdays, June through September. Just go into the low red brick building on the left at the end of Kok Road and request a tour. If you've chosen a really hot day to ride through the muck, you will enjoy walking into one of the plant's coolers, which are kept at a constant thirty-six degrees Fahrenheit. The plant also has an ice-making machine that runs twenty-four hours a day in summer. This machine makes 800 pounds of ice every ten minutes; that's sixty tons per day! It is also interesting to see how quickly and efficiently vegetables are washed and packed for shipment across the country.

As you continue your ride, gliding over the ribbons of black road slicing through the flat, seemingly endless fields of multiple shades of green, you will notice ditches crisscrossing the fields. The Celeryville Conservancy District maintains more than 7 miles of these irrigation ditches, and there is a small reservoir behind a dike not far southwest of the intersection of OH–103 and Base Line Road.

In summer you also will see a lot of human activity in the fields. About 75 percent of the field hands in this area are Mexican–Americans from Texas. These migrant workers live in small labor camps visible along OH–103.

After the town of Plymouth, halfway through your ride, the terrain becomes slightly rolling and you will see more trees as you cross the North Branch Huron River and several streams. None of this ride, however, is difficult. You should have plenty of energy left afterward for a refreshing dip in the pool at Willard Park.

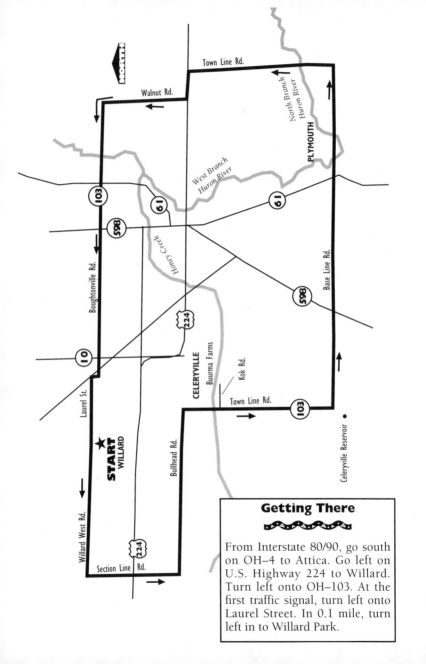

NORTH

Town Line Rd.

Walnut Rd.

North Branch Huron River

PLYMOUTH

West Branch Huron River

103

61

61

598

Boughtonville Rd.

Honey Creek

Base Line Rd.

598

224

10

Buurma Farms

CELERYVILLE

Kok Rd.

Laurel St.

Town Line Rd.

103

★ START
WILLARD

Bullhead Rd.

Celeryville Reservoir

Willard West Rd.

224

Section Line Rd.

Getting There

From Interstate 80/90, go south on OH–4 to Attica. Go left on U.S. Highway 224 to Willard. Turn left onto OH–103. At the first traffic signal, turn left onto Laurel Street. In 0.1 mile, turn left in to Willard Park.

DIREC-TIONS at a glance

0.0	Turn left out of Willard park onto Laurel Street.
0.3	Road becomes Willard West after Washburn Street.
2.3	Turn left at stop sign at T intersection onto Section Line Road.

3.1 Cross U.S. Highway 224 at stop sign.

3.9 Turn left at stop sign onto Bullhead Road.

6.5 Turn right at stop sign onto OH–103 and ride through Celeryville.

8.0 Turn left onto Kok Road to visit Buurma Farms.

8.3 Buurma Farms vegetable-packing plant tour. To continue ride, turn around and retrace your route to OH–103.

8.6 Turn left onto OH–103.

9.7 Turn left at stop sign at T intersection onto Base Line Road.

12.0 Road name becomes West Broadway at Plymouth corporation limit sign.

13.0 Cross OH–61/98 at traffic signal.

13.1 Continue straight onto narrow road into the country (don't curve right with OH–603). Road becomes East Main Street.

14.5 Road becomes Base Line Road.

14.9 Turn left onto Townline Road/TR 111.

15.5 Cautiously cross rough railroad tracks at the bottom of hill.

17.4 Turn left at stop sign at T intersection onto U.S. Highway 224.

17.9 Turn right onto Walnut Road.

19.3 Turn left at stop sign onto Boughtonville Road/OH–103.

23.1 Cross OH–99/Tiffin Road at traffic signal (traffic picks up here).

23.2 Go under railroad overpass. *Caution:* road narrows under bridge.

23.3 Turn right onto Ash Street.

23.4 Turn left onto Laurel Street.

24.0 At traffic signal, jog right, then immediately left to cross Main Street and continue on Laurel.

24.1 Turn left into Willard Park to end ride.

The Lowdown on Upper Sandusky

Number of miles:	21.4
Approximate pedaling time:	2.5 hours
Terrain:	Gently rolling
Surface:	Some rough stretches, including a couple short unpaved segments
Traffic:	Light, except on federal and state routes
Things to see:	Indian Mill State Memorial, Parker Covered Bridge, Chief Tarhe monument, beautiful old houses in Upper Sandusky
Facilities:	Restaurants, stores, a bike shop in Upper Sandusky; water and restrooms at Bicentennial Park

This ride takes in the gently rolling lands along the Sandusky River and the nearly flat fields of corn and soybeans on what was once one of nine Indian reservations in Ohio. The reservation was home to the Wyandot tribe for whom Wyandot County was named.

The Wyandots, under the leadership of Chief Tarhe ("The Crane") were among the tribes that signed the Treaty of GreenVille in 1795. Tarhe was a man of his word, and when the great Shawnee leader Tecumseh pushed him to ally the Wyandots with the British against the Americans in the War of 1812, he refused. Instead Tarhe and other Wyandots took up arms and joined the American forces.

Despite the loyal service of the Wyandots and other Indians,

in 1817 the United States decided to settle the tribes on smaller, separate reservations. The government wanted to make more land open to white settlement, so it proposed three reservations apiece for the Ottawas and Shawnees and one each for the Wyandots, Senecas and Delawares.

The Wyandots signed the treaty under protest and were moved to a 12-mile-square block of land with Fort Ferree (Upper Sandusky) at its center. The Wyandots also received an annuity of $4,000 for their loss of land in the move to the reservation, and an indemnity of $4,319.39 for property losses sustained in the War of 1812. The United States also promised never to seek a surrender of Indian territory and pledged a blacksmith and a saw- and gristmill to the Wyandots.

The mill was built in 1820 on the Sandusky River about 3.5 miles north of Upper Sandusky. This mill remained in operation until the Wyandots, giving in to increasing white encroachment and pressure from the U.S. government, moved to another reservation in Kansas in 1843. In the early 1860s, the mill was replaced by a new mill that is now the Indian Mill State Memorial, located 2.4 miles into your ride. A small shady grove just across the river from the mill is a wonderful picnic site and the best place from which to take a photo of the mill.

You'll cross the 1873 Parker Covered Bridge on a shady stretch at Mile 8.4. In 1991 vandals torched the bridge and one end of it fell into the Sandusky River. Through the work of county officials and local historical society volunteers, the bridge was restored and reopened to traffic in 1992.

Slow down on Township Highway 35, lest you miss a monument to the great Chief Tarhe. Look for some evergreen shrubbery at Mile 9, and there you will see a marble memorial inscribed "Chief Tarhe—Distinguished Wyandot chief and loyal American. Died here in Cranetown. Erected by Tarhe Tribe 1915."

The unpaved portions of this ride are between your crossings of OH–53 and U.S. Highway 23. Neither stretch is longer than .7 mile.

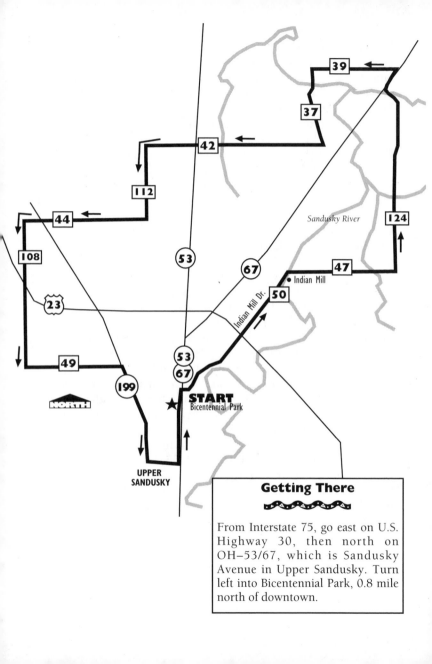

39

37

42

112

124

44

Sandusky River

108

67

47

53

50

• Indian Mill

23

Indian Mill Dr.

53
67

NORTH

49

199

★ **START**
Bicentennial Park

**UPPER
SANDUSKY**

Getting There

From Interstate 75, go east on U.S.
Highway 30, then north on
OH–53/67, which is Sandusky
Avenue in Upper Sandusky. Turn
left into Bicentennial Park, 0.8 mile
north of downtown.

DIREC-TIONS at a glance

0.0	Turn left out of Bicentennial Park onto North Sandusky Avenue/OH–53/67.
0.3	Turn right onto Indian Mill Drive/Wyandot County Highway 50.
1.5	Cross U.S. Highway 23 at stop sign. Use caution; busy divided highway.

2.2 Turn right at stop sign at T intersection onto CH 47 and go downhill.

2.4 Indian Mill State Memorial is on right before metal bridge crossing the Sandusky River. To leave the mill, turn right at the Y intersection to continue on CH 47 across the river.

6.7 Turn right at stop sign at T intersection onto OH–67. Use caution.

7.1 Turn left onto CH 39.

8.3 Turn left at stop sign at T intersection onto Township Highway 40.

8.4 Cross 1873 Parker Covered Bridge.

8.7 Turn left at stop sign at T intersection onto TH 37.

9.0 Chief Tarhe monument is on right.

9.4 Turn right on TH 42.

11.1 Cross OH–53 at stop sign. Road is unpaved after OH–53 crossing.

11.8 Turn left onto paved narrow TH 112.

12.8 Turn right at stop sign at T intersection onto CH 44.

14.5 Cross rough railroad tracks. Use caution.

14.6 Turn left onto CH 108. Road is very rough, then turns to gravel.

15.3 Road becomes paved.

15.6 Turn right at stop sign at T intersection onto CH 47 and cross bridges over U.S. Highway 23.

15.8 Turn left onto CH 108.

17.1 Turn left at stop sign at T intersection onto TH 49, again crossing a bridge over U.S. Highway 23.

18.5 Cross railroad tracks.

18.8 Turn right at stop sign onto OH–199.
20.2 Turn left to continue on OH–199/West Wyandot Street.
20.6 Turn left at traffic signal on North Sandusky Avenue/ OH–53/67 opposite the Wyandot County Courthouse.
21.4 Turn left into Bicentennial Park to end ride.

Don't feel that your enjoyment of this ride must end when you get back to Upper Sandusky. West Wyandot Street/OH–199 west of town, and North Sandusky Avenue/OH–53/67 south of Bicentennial Park, have many large attractive old houses worth admiring.

Bogie, Bacall, and Bicycles

Number of miles:	17.4
Approximate pedaling time:	2 hours
Terrain:	Rolling
Traffic:	Light
Things to see:	Malabar Farm State Park, Pleasant Valley
Facilities:	Restrooms, water, limited snacks, bike parking, and primitive camping at Malabar Farm State Park; youth hostel just outside the state park

Louis Bromfield was a Pulitzer Prize-winning author (for the novel *Early Autumn*). Lucky for us, he was much more. He was a Hollywood screenwriter and naturalist who loved the land and pioneered radical farming techniques such as contour plowing.

In 1939 he bought four worn-out farms in Richland County's Pleasant Valley. Using his ideas on agriculture, he transformed Malabar Farm into a farming showplace. Many of the country's rich and famous visited the Bromfield estate. He even hosted a wedding away from prying eyes for Lauren Bacall and Humphrey Bogart.

Bromfield knew what he was doing when he moved his family to Richland County. The area is beautiful and hilly, and at that time was pretty isolated. This route stays in the valley, paralleling creeks, and away from the most difficult hills.

The state park itself has a lot to see. The Big House is a 32-room country farmhouse mansion built by Bromfield. In 1945 Bogie and Bacall were married in front of the twin staircase and

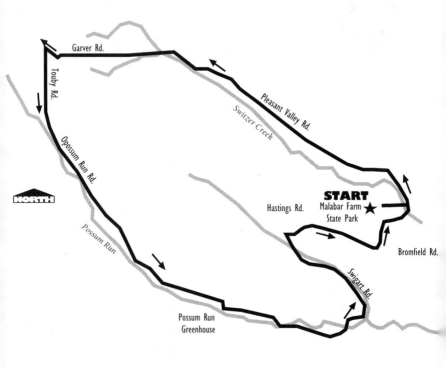

Garver Rd.

Touby Rd.

Opossum Run Rd.

Switzer Creek

Pleasant Valley Rd.

NORTH

Hastings Rd.

START
Malabar Farm
State Park

Bromfield Rd.

Possum Run

Swigart Rd.

Possum Run
Greenhouse

Getting There

From Interstate 71, take OH–13 north. Make a right onto Hanley Road immediately after going under the interstate. After 2 miles, turn right onto Little Washington Road. Bear left onto Pleasant Valley Road and follow it for 7 miles to the entrance of Malabar Farm State Park on Bromfield Road.

DIRECTIONS at a glance

0.0	Go back out driveway from parking lot.
0.3	Turn left onto Bromfield Road.
0.3	Turn left at stop sign at **T** intersection onto Pleasant Valley Road.
4.7	Turn left at **Y** intersection onto Garver Road. Caution: gravel.
6.1	Turn left at stop sign onto Touby Road.
7.0	Turn left at stop sign onto O'Possum Run Road.
10.9	Turn left at **Y** intersection to continue on O'Possum Run Road.
13.1	Turn left onto Swigart Road.
14.8	Turn right onto Hastings Road. *Caution:* gravel.
16.1	Turn left at **Y** intersection onto Bromfield Road.
16.3	State park camping and picnic areas are on right.
16.7	Big House is on left.
17.0	Malabar Farm Hostel is on right.
17.1	Turn left into state park driveway.
17.4	End ride in Big House parking lot.

honeymooned on the farm. Guided tours of the house are given year-round. Wagon rides on the grounds are also offered, and many of the farm buildings are open for visitors to walk through. One of the smaller barns has a discovery center with hands-on displays about farming.

You'll begin this ride in the Big House parking lot; make your way out to Pleasant Valley Road and turn left. The road is aptly named, as it has only gentle hills and passes by beautiful farm scenery. Your next turn, onto Garver Road at Mile 4.7, is concealed by a small rise. It is immediately after the intersection with Hastings–Newville Road. Garver has a lot of gravel on it at this intersection, so be careful. The turn onto O'Possum Run Road is at the bottom of a short, steep hill, requiring vigilance as well.

Your eyes will get a real treat at Mile 11.6. Possum Run Greenhouse on the right has a beautiful floral display. Your tip-off to your next turn in this gently rolling terrain will be a church and a small bridge over a creek. Swigart Road is just before these landmarks.

Beware of the gravel at the turn onto Hastings Road. Hastings will take you through a beautiful stretch of woods. You'll pass through a tunnel of green in the summer, and a riot of color in the fall.

You'll know you've nearly finished your journey when you reach the Bromfield Road turn. This pleasant road will take you past the state park's camping and picnic areas, then by the Big House. You'll see the Malabar Farm Hostel on the left just .1 mile before the state park driveway.

Emerald Necklace

Number of miles:	18.4
Approximate pedaling time:	2 hours
Terrain:	Rolling, with a couple steep hills
Surface:	Paved multi-use trail and residential streets
Things to see:	Cleveland Metroparks, Rocky River, waterfalls, nature preserves
Facilities:	Water, toilets, and picnic facilities throughout metroparks; food at Quarry Rock Cafe at Wallace Lake, and within a few blocks on major crossroads; bike shop at 27093 Bagley Road in Olmsted Township.

This ride may well be the jewel of this book, combining, as it does, big-city hustle with country quiet.

In 1917 Cleveland established its metroparks to provide green space and preserve the natural valleys of the area for residents in the Greater Cleveland area. The first park commission set up a plan to acquire land that would encircle Cleveland. They envisioned interconnecting parkways running throughout the area, offering great ease of accessibility to Clevelanders. Thus a city of more than 500,000 people now has a network of more than 100 miles of parkway and 45-plus miles of multi-use trails on more than 19,000 acres that make up twelve reservations and the Cleveland Metroparks Zoo. It is known as the Emerald Necklace.

45

The parkways are restricted in speed and closed to trucks, so it is relatively safe to cycle on them. For the joy of weaving in and out of woods, next to athletic fields, picnic areas, lakes and tumbling waterfalls, and over rustic bridges crossing rushing rivers, stick to the multi-use path as much as possible. Even without motorized traffic, the path requires some vigilance, for it has a capricious way of crossing and recrossing the parkways. At major crossroads, though, users of the path have their own button to trip the traffic signals.

This route is a loop that includes some non-parkway streets. You'll pass through suburban residential areas and a light industrial area. Don't think of this as a disadvantage, though; after all, it accentuates the fact that just a step away from everyday suburban Cleveland is a polished jewel.

The natural wonders of your ride begin immediately, as you look down on a waterfall from a bridge on the right at North Quarry Road only .1 mile after starting. Then there's Berea Falls Overlook, a picturesque stop on the right at Mile 1.5.

Be prepared for a short, but steep, climb out of the valley at Mile 3.9. For the next 7 miles you will be on city streets. The highlight of this off-the-parkway segment is Brookside's John A. Polonye Recreation Center, including a water park, on the left about 8 miles into the ride.

When you reach Big Creek Parkway, you will get back on the multi-use path by crossing to the middle of the road, then turning right onto the green strip in the middle of the parkway. The rest of your ride will be on the path. A restful place to consider stopping on this segment is Lake Isaac Waterfowl Sanctuary, where you might spot ducks, geese, herons, and egrets.

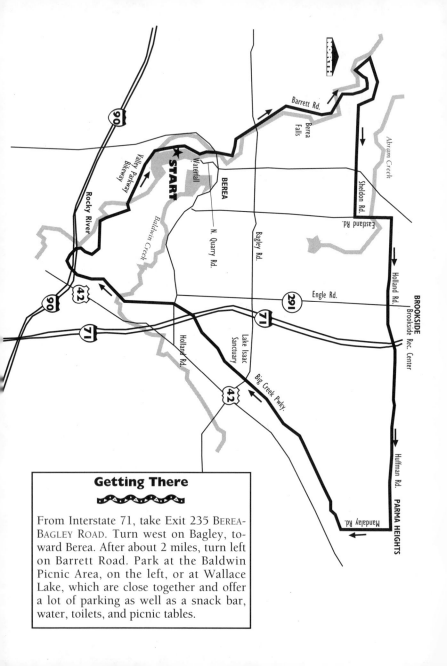

Getting There

From Interstate 71, take Exit 235 BEREA-BAGLEY ROAD. Turn west on Bagley, toward Berea. After about 2 miles, turn left on Barrett Road. Park at the Baldwin Picnic Area, on the left, or at Wallace Lake, which are close together and offer a lot of parking as well as a snack bar, water, toilets, and picnic tables.

DIREC-TIONS at a glance

0.0 Go north, back toward Bagley Road, on the multi-use trail.

0.1 Cross North Quarry Road at stop sign and remain on the path to the right of the parkway.

0.6 Continue straight on path where you have the option of going right.

1.1 Cross Bagley Road at traffic signal to continue into the Rocky River Reservation.

1.4 Turn right on Barrett Road after traveling beneath two highway bridges.

1.5 Turn right into Berea Falls Reservation. Berea Falls Overlook is on right.

1.6 Cross road to continue on path.

2.0 Go down short steep hill.

2.2 Cross wooden bridge over river.

2.6 Willow Bend Picnic Area is on right across parkway.

3.8 Cross river on wooden bridge.

3.9 Turn right at stop sign onto Spafford Road, cross the parkway, and go up hill.

4.0 Cross bridge over river and go up steep hill.

4.1 Turn right at stop sign at T intersection on Ruple Parkway.

4.9 Road becomes Grayton Road.

5.0 Turn left onto Sheldon Road at yellow flasher.

5.8 Cross OH–237 at traffic signal.

6.0 Cross four sets of railroad tracks.

6.3 Turn left at traffic signal before railroad overpass onto Eastland Road.

6.7 Turn right at traffic signal onto Holland Road.

6.9 Cross railroad tracks.

7.1 Carefully cross single, then double, railroad tracks.

9.2 Cross railroad tracks.

9.9 Cross West 130th Street at traffic signal into Parma Heights. Street becomes to Huffman Road.

10.4 Turn right onto Mandalay Drive (fifth right after 130th, opposite Greenbriar Junior High School).

11.0 At traffic signal, cross to center of Big Creek Parkway and turn right onto multi-use path.

13.2 Cross Bagley Road at traffic signal and veer slightly left to continue on path.

14.4 Cross road, then cross again to continue on the path.

14.6 Lake Isaac Waterfowl Sanctuary is on right.

15.0 Cross parkway to remain on path.

15.1 Picnic area is on right.

15.4 Cross parkway to remain on path.

15.7 Cross Whitney Road, then cross parkway to remain on path.

16.2 Turn right at stop sign at T intersection after crossing Valley Parkway, and immediately go under highway overpass.

17.3 Enter Mill Stream Run Reservation. Cross wooden bridge, then cross parkway to remain on path.

17.9 Restrooms on right at start of Parcourse fitness trail.

18.3 Baldwin Lake Viewing Area (metal tower for observing wildlife) is on right.

18.4 Turn left, crossing parkway, to enter Wallace Lake parking lot, or veer left to Baldwin Picnic parking lot to end ride.

Towpath Trek

Distance:	14.5 miles
Approximate pedaling time:	2 hours
Terrain:	Flat
Surface:	Finely crushed limestone multi-use trail
Things to see:	Cuyahoga Valley National Recreation Area, Cuyahoga Valley Scenic Railway, Ohio & Erie Canal Towpath Trail, Cuyahoga River
Facilities:	Food in Independence, Boston, and Peninsula; toilets, water, and picnic areas along the trail; Century Cycles bike shop with rentals at Peninsula

Running through downtown Cleveland to Lake Erie is the Cuyahoga River, which gained notoriety in the 1970s, when it was so polluted it caught fire.

Ohio has cleaned up the lake and the river since then. But recently the Cuyahoga has caught fire again—this time in the hearts of those who love nature and history. It has been wrapped up in a package and laid at the doorstep of the largest metropolitan area in Ohio in the form of the Cuyahoga Valley National Recreation Area.

The first stretch of the Ohio & Erie Canal was built adjacent to the river from 1825 to 1827. From its terminus on Lake Erie it rose 395 feet en route to Akron. The canal was a boon to development, bringing prosperity to Cleveland and Akron. The building of a railroad through the valley in 1880 helped bring about the

51

demise of the canal, but contributed to the growth of the cities.

These two modes of transportation are no longer essential to the commerce of northeastern Ohio, but combine to provide myriad recreational opportunities. The towpath along the old canal is now a multi-use path perfect for pedestrians and cyclists, and the rails are now traveled by tourist trains.

The crushed-limestone Towpath Trail extends nearly 20 miles from Lock 39 on Rockside Road in Independence to Indian Mound Trailhead north of Akron. The Cuyahoga Valley Scenic Railroad's end points are Rockside Road in Independence and Quaker Square in downtown Akron. Both travel through woods, fields and wetlands, offering possible views of wildlife such as deer, beaver, coyotes, hawks, herons and waterfowl, in addition to the ruins of the canal.

This ride combines train and trail between Independence and Peninsula. The railway offers a "Bike and Hike" excursion. You can buy an all-day ticket, which allows you to flag down the train at several stops any time throughout the day, or a one-way ticket. You need not even bring your own bike, as rentals are available in Peninsula.

We suggest buying a one-way ticket and boarding the train at Rockside Road. The conductor will direct you to the baggage car so you can load your bike if you have it with you. Then find your seat and relax for the journey to Peninsula. A conductor will narrate the history of the Cuyahoga Valley and explain the passing views, and there may be a park ranger on board to answer questions.

When you get off the train in Peninsula, turn left on the road outside the depot. When you turn left across the double railroad tracks, you'll see a maroon building with public restrooms. From here you can walk about a block on a marked pedestrian walkway to downtown, where you can get a bite to eat or rent a bike. Start your ride from the public restroom by going left through the parking lot. Signs will point out the trail. This ride takes you to the right, but you could add up to 13 miles to your ride by going left.

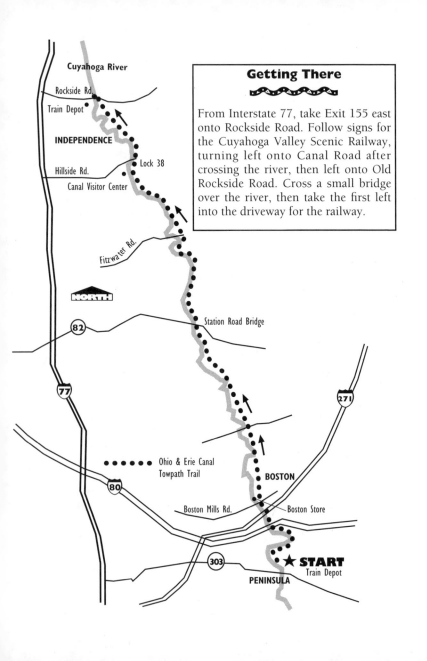

Cuyahoga River

Rockside Rd.

Train Depot

INDEPENDENCE

Lock 38

Hillside Rd.

Canal Visitor Center

Fitzwater Rd.

NORTH

82

77

Station Road Bridge

271

● ● ● ● ● ● Ohio & Erie Canal
Towpath Trail

80

BOSTON

Boston Mills Rd.

Boston Store

303

★ **START**
Train Depot

PENINSULA

Getting There

From Interstate 77, take Exit 155 east onto Rockside Road. Follow signs for the Cuyahoga Valley Scenic Railway, turning left onto Canal Road after crossing the river, then left onto Old Rockside Road. Cross a small bridge over the river, then take the first left into the driveway for the railway.

DIRECTIONS at a glance

0.0	Turn left from Peninsula train depot.
0.1	Turn left and cross two railroad tracks. (Maroon building on the left houses restrooms and a drinking fountain.)
0.1	Turn left and go through the trailhead parking lot to gain access to the Towpath Trail.

0.2 Turn right onto the trail.

2.5 Turn left to stay on trail, and go through Boston. The Boston Store museum is on the left.

4.5 Cross Highland Road (caution: fast cross traffic).

7.1 Turn left if you wish to go to Station Road Bridge trailhead. Otherwise, continue straight.

7.2 Cross Pinery Dam and Gate, which allows water from the river into the canal north of this point.

10.3 Cross Fitzwater Road (caution: cross traffic).

11.8 Canal Visitor Center is on left; Lock 38 is on right.

11.8 Cross Hillside Road.

13.6 Turn left and go up into Rockside Road trailhead parking lot.

13.7 Turn right onto Rockside Road.

13.7 Turn left at traffic signal onto Canal Road.

13.8 Turn left onto Old Rockside Road.

14.0 Turn left into railway driveway.

14.4 End ride in Cuyahoga Valley Scenic Railway parking lot.

At Mile 2.5, you'll pass through the formerly bustling canal town of Boston. If you've bought the all-day ticket there is train access here. Stop at the Boston Store museum if you are interested in the craft of building canal boats. Should you be thirsty or hungry there is a store within sight of the trail to the left on Boston Mills Road.

Mile 7.1 brings your second chance to flag down the train. Turn left and cross the 1881 Station Road Bridge, which has an unusual wooden-block deck. Turn left just off the bridge to enter the trailhead, where parking, portable toilets, picnic tables, and train access are available.

The Canal Visitor Center, at Mile 11.8, offers another chance to flag down the train. There are picnic facilities, water, portable toilets, and bike parking outside, and a museum with restrooms and water inside. Lock 38 is on the right of the trail, opposite the visitor center. Lock demonstrations are given on weekend afternoons, so there is likely to be a lot of pedestrian traffic then.

When you reach the Rockside Road trailhead parking lot, you will need to make your way to the surface streets for .8 mile in order to reach the railway parking area and end your adventure.

Note that the mile markers along the trail won't match your odometer. The trail is marked according to the mileage along the old canal starting from Lake Erie, even though the trail itself doesn't extend that far north yet.

Geneva Convention

Number of miles:	28.7
Approximate pedaling time:	3 hours
Terrain:	Mostly flat, with a few ridges and a short climb from the Grand River
Traffic:	Geneva-on-the-Lake and roads around Geneva State Park are very busy during summer weekends
Surface:	Includes intermittent, mostly short, unpaved stretches
Things to see:	Ree's Drug Store and Soda Fountain, wineries, covered bridges, Ohio's first summer resort, and Geneva State Park
Facilities:	Restaurants and stores in Geneva and Geneva-on-the-Lake; picnic facilities, water, and restrooms at Harpersfield MetroPark; beach, picnic facilities, water, restrooms, marina store, and camping at Geneva State Park

You will be happy to give more than your name, rank, and serial number by the time you're done with this fun-filled ride. Three wineries, an old-time soda fountain, swimming in Lake Erie, a lively summer resort, and two of Ashtabula County's famous covered bridges are all on this tour.

This trip features a convention of Genevas: the city of Geneva, the village of Geneva-on-the-Lake, and Geneva State Park. You'll start and end your ride in the little city of Geneva, which has a thriving downtown with several cafes and an old-

fashioned pharmacy with a real soda fountain. Ohio's first summer resort, Geneva-on-the-Lake, has only 1,600 year-round residents but attracts about 280,000 tourists every summer. Geneva State Park fills every summer weekend with campers, boaters, swimmers, and anglers who enjoy being on Lake Erie.

This is the tour for you if sampling some award-winning Ohio wines tickles your fancy. You will ride by some of the vineyards and wineries that dot this region of Ohio. Lake Erie and the mostly flat topography are the reasons for the expanses of grapevines. This shallowest of the Great Lakes moderates the weather on its southern shores, staving off the coldest of winter weather and providing an average of 193 frost-free days a year. The plateaulike land with intermittent sandy ridges also provides the good drainage necessary to viticulture.

You can visit three wineries on this ride: Cantwell's Old Mill Winery, in a mill built in the 1860s, in Geneva; Ferrante Winery & Ristorante, an attractive new place among the vines 4 miles south of Geneva; and the Old Firehouse Winery, in Geneva-on-the-Lake's first fire station, 18.7 miles into the ride. All offer winery tours and tasting sessions; Ferrante and the Old Firehouse also have full-service restaurants.

Geneva-on-the-Lake got its start as a summer resort in the early 1900s, when some of the wealthiest families in America—including the Firestones, Fords and Rockefellers—started coming to camp along Lake Erie. By 1905, more than fifty cottages and twenty boarding houses had sprung up, luring wealthy vacationers from Cleveland and Youngstown, Ohio, and Pittsburgh, Pennsylvania. By the 1930s, middle-class families were coming to enjoy a lakeside vacation, too. Several big ballrooms were built along the lake, and famous bands on tour came to town to play for the summer crowd.

No longer are the ballrooms or big bands in Geneva-on-the-Lake, but from Memorial Day to Labor Day the town is full of families renting cottages or motel rooms for a week at a time. Not surprisingly, traffic through town in the summer is a bit busy and slow-moving, but there are plenty of attractions, in-

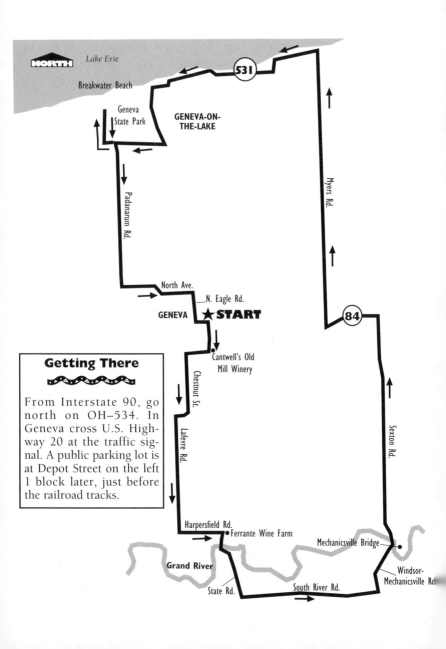

NORTH

Lake Erie

Breakwater Beach

Geneva State Park

GENEVA-ON-THE-LAKE

531

Myers Rd.

Padanarum Rd.

North Ave.

N. Eagle Rd.

GENEVA ★ **START**

Cantwell's Old Mill Winery

Chestnut St.

Lafevre Rd.

84

Sexton Rd.

Harpersfield Rd.
Ferrante Wine Farm

Mechanicsville Bridge

Grand River

Windsor-Mechanicsville Rd

State Rd.

South River Rd.

Getting There

From Interstate 90, go north on OH–534. In Geneva cross U.S. Highway 20 at the traffic signal. A public parking lot is at Depot Street on the left 1 block later, just before the railroad tracks.

DIREC-TIONS at a glance

0.0 From the parking lot, go left (east) on Depot Street.

0.0 Turn right onto Broadway/OH–534.

0.1 Cross U.S. Highway 20 at traffic signal (Ree's Drug Store and Soda Fountain is on the southwest corner).

0.4 Cantwell's Old Mill Winery is on the left.

0.4 Turn right onto West Liberty Street.

0.7 Turn left at stop sign onto Chestnut Street.

0.8 Cross railroad tracks.

1.6 Turn right at stop sign at T intersection onto OH–84.

1.8 Turn left onto Lafevre Road.

2.9 Cross over Interstate 90 on bridge. Road gets very rough and soon becomes unpaved.

3.5 Turn left onto OH–307. *Caution:* busy especially on weekends.

3.9 Ferrante Winery is on left.

4.2 Turn right onto Harpersfield Road.

4.5 Cross Grand River on 1868 Harpersfield Covered Bridge just past Harpersfield MetroPark.

4.6 Turn left onto unmarked state road immediately after crossing bridge.

5.0 Cross OH–534 to continue on state road, which is unpaved shortly after the intersection.

5.4 Turn left at stop sign onto unmarked, very rough South River Road.

7.3 Turn left at stop sign at T intersection onto unmarked, paved Windsor–Mechanicsville Road.

8.0 The 1867 Mechanicsville Covered Bridge is on the right.

8.1 Veer left to continue on Windsor–Mechanicsville Road.

9.0 Cross OH–307 to continue on Sexton Road.

11.5 Turn left at stop sign at T intersection onto OH–84.

12.4 Turn right onto South Myers Road.

12.6 Cross railroad tracks.

13.2 Cross U.S. Highway 20 at stop sign to continue on North Myers Road.

13.6 Cross two extremely uneven railroad tracks.

16.6 Turn left at stop sign at T intersection onto OH–531.

17.9 Geneva Township. Park is on right.

18.2 Turn left at stop sign at T intersection to continue on OH–531 and enter Geneva-on-the-Lake.

18.7 Turn right to go to Old Firehouse Winery.

19.0 Road veers left and becomes OH–534.

19.3 Veer left to remain on paved OH–534.

20.2 Turn right onto Park Road to enter Geneva State Park.

21.7 Turn right for Breakwater Beach.

21.8 Breakwater Beach parking lot. To leave retrace your steps and turn right onto OH–531. Turn right to go to Old Firehouse.

22.6 Turn right at stop sign onto Padanarum Road.

24.7 Turn left onto unpaved North Avenue.

27.4 Geneva city limits.

27.9 Road is paved.

28.0 Turn right onto North Eagle Road.

28.5 Cross two sets railroad tracks.

28.5 Turn left onto Depot Road.

28.7 Turn left into municipal parking lot to end ride.

cluding a pretty township park, an amusement park with water slides, arcades, restaurants galore, and gift shops.

For a more restful experience, bring a picnic lunch and spend some time in Harpersfield MetroPark at Mile 4.5. This beautiful park along the Grand River offers a great view of the river and the renovated 1868 Harpersfield Covered Bridge (at 228 feet, it's the longest in Ohio). You'll have to climb out of the river valley after crossing the bridge.

Another break from commercialism can be found at Geneva State Park, which has a public beach with lifeguards. The beach, at Mile 21.8, is nice enough, but don't expect modern amenities here. There are bike racks but only portable toilets; modern restrooms are in the campground and at the marina elsewhere in the park.

Bridges to the Past

Number of miles:	20.5 miles
Approximate pedaling time:	2 hours
Terrain:	Flat to rolling, with some short, steep climbs
Traffic:	Generally light, except on federal and state routes, and during the annual Covered Bridge Festival
Surface:	Long stretches of unpaved roads
Things to see:	Lake Erie, Conneaut Railroad Museum, covered bridges, and vineyards
Facilities:	Restaurants and stores in Conneaut; beach, picnic facilities, restrooms, water, and snack shop at Conneaut Township Park; restrooms, water, and snacks at Buccia Vineyard (Buccia Vineyard also has bed-and-breakfast inn accommodations)

With more than 2,000 covered bridges, Ohio once had more than any other state in the union. Even today, with 136 covered bridges, it is second only to Pennsylvania. Ashtabula County, in the state's northeast corner on the border with Pennsylvania, has taken the cause of the covered bridge to heart. It has fourteen covered bridges, two of which were built in the 1980s. Nowhere else in Ohio can you see covered bridges more lovingly restored or appreciated.

Many of the roads on this route are unpaved and every creek seems to be spanned by a picturesque covered bridge, so it is

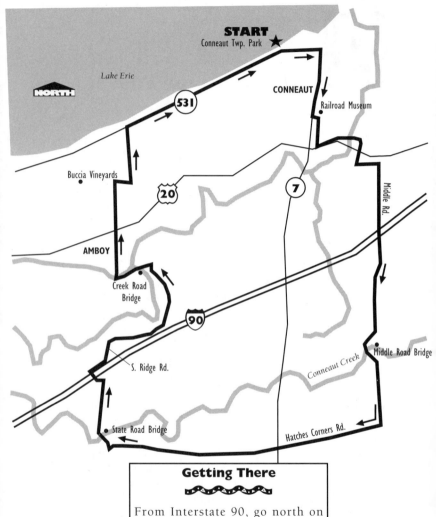

START
Conneaut Twp. Park

Lake Erie

NORTH

531

CONNEAUT

Railroad Museum

Buccia Vineyards

20

7

Middle Rd.

AMBOY

Creek Road Bridge

90

S. Ridge Rd.

Middle Road Bridge

Conneaut Creek

State Road Bridge

Hatches Corners Rd.

Getting There

From Interstate 90, go north on OH–7 into Conneaut. Turn left onto OH–531 (Lake Road). After about .2 mile, turn right into Conneaut Township Park. Park in lot overlooking Lake Erie.

0.0 From parking lot, exit park the same way you came in.

0.2 Turn left at stop sign at T intersection onto Lake Road/OH–531.

0.3 Turn right onto Mill Street (follow railroad museum sign).

1.1 Cross very uneven railroad tracks.

1.1 Turn left onto Depot Street.

1.1 Turn right onto Sandusky Street.

1.4 Cross two sets railroad tracks.

1.6 Turn left at stop sign at T intersection onto Main Street.

2.0 Cross railroad tracks, then bridge across Conneaut Creek.

2.4 Take second right onto Dorman Road.

2.6 Turn left onto High Street.

2.8 Turn right at stop sign onto very rough Middle Road.

3.7 Cross bridge over Interstate 90.

3.9 .Unpaved road begins.

5.1 Turn right at stop sign at T intersection onto South Ridge Road.

5.3 Turn left to continue on Middle Road (immediate downhill).

5.4 Cross Middle Road Covered Bridge.

6.6 Turn right at stop sign onto paved Hatches Corners Road.

10.4 Turn right at stop sign at T intersection at bottom of hill onto State Road.

10.6 Cross State Road Covered Bridge, then climb out of valley on rough surface.

11.1 Road is unpaved.

11.4 Turn left at stop sign at T intersection onto unmarked road.

11.6 Go under Interstate 90 overpass.

11.7 Turn right at stop sign at T intersection onto South Ridge Road.

12.9 Turn left at stop sign at T intersection onto unmarked

Keefus Road (bridge over Interstate 90 is to immediate right of intersection).

13.9 Turn left onto gravel Creek Road and go downhill.

14.1 Cross Creek Road Covered Bridge.

14.4 Turn right at stop sign onto paved South Amboy Road.

15.1 Cross U.S. Highway 20 at traffic light to continue on North Amboy Road.

15.3 Cross two railroad tracks. Note that road is rough after tracks.

15.7 Turn left at stop sign at T intersection onto Gore Road.

15.9 Cautiously cross two badly angled railroad tracks.

16.1 Turn right into Buccia Vineyard. To leave, turn left onto Gore Road.

16.2 Cautiously cross two badly angled railroad tracks.

16.6 Turn left onto unmarked road.

16.8 Cross two sets very uneven railroad tracks.

17.4 Turn right at stop sign at T intersection onto Lake Road/OH–531.

20.1 Turn left to enter Conneaut Township Park (second entrance).

20.2 Turn left at Y intersection to descend to beach house, concession stand, and beach. To leave beach, walk your bike back the way you came in.

20.3 Take first left and walk up hill.

20.5 Turn left into overlook parking lot to end ride.

---

easy to believe you've been transported back in time. This ride is best made on a fat-tired bike, because of the rough surfaces. Don't let the road surfaces dissuade you from doing this tour, however. The combination of flat terrain along Lake Erie and rolling terrain south of Interstate 90, the meticulously maintained covered bridges, and a small, rustic winery make for a pleasant afternoon of cycling.

On this ride you will cross the Middle Road Bridge (Mile 5.4), which was built in 1868 and restored by the county with the help of volunteers in 1984; the State Road Bridge (Mile 10.6), which was built in 1983; and the 124-foot-long Creek Road Bridge (Mile 14.1), whose history is unknown.

Begin your ride in Conneaut Township Park on a hill over-looking Lake Erie. Just a few blocks away, you'll pass an old rail-road depot, which is now a small museum. You can't miss the huge steam locomotive on display outside the depot.

Just after the Middle Road Bridge on the right is a miniature horse farm, which will help take your mind off the climb out of the creek valley.

Three-quarters of the way into the ride, you will cross a pair of railroad tracks at a very bad angle. Be extra careful here! Just .2 mile farther, you can relax at the rustic Buccia Vineyard. Try a selection of this small family establishment's wines while enjoying a snack of bread and cheese or a picnic lunch that you've brought along. The Bucci family even runs a bed-and-breakfast inn, if you want to spend some more time in Ohio's Lake Erie wine country and covered bridge capital.

The Ashtabula County Covered Bridge Festival is held in Jefferson on the second weekend of October. During the festival, many folks drive a marked tour of the area's covered bridges that includes the bridges on this ride. Although fall is a wonderful time to take this ride, it probably would be best to avoid it during the festival because of the heavy traffic.

At Holmes with the Amish

Number of miles:	28.1 miles
Approximate pedaling time:	3.5 hours
Terrain:	Rolling, with a few steep hills
Surface:	Sometimes rough with some gravel stretches
Traffic:	Can be heavy in towns and on federal and state routes
Things to see:	Beautiful rolling farmland; Amish farms, craft shops, and restaurants; cheese factories; Central Ohio Railroad; villages of Sugarcreek, Charm, and Berlin
Facilities:	Food, water, and restrooms in Sugarcreek, Charm, and Berlin; Charm Bicycle Shop in Charm

No need to count yourself lucky to see one or two horse-drawn buggies on this ride. Holmes County has more Amish people than Lancaster County, Pennsylvania. In fact it has the largest concentration of Amish in the world. On this ride, you will see the Amish everywhere: On the road in buggies and on bicycles, in the stores, even at McDonald's.

The Amish believe service to God is the reason for being. They believe that any technology that does not enhance their relationship to God should not be used. Cars are not considered evil, but a fast-paced life that tends to shuffle God to the background is to be avoided.

The Amish people's life of faith has some surprising benefits

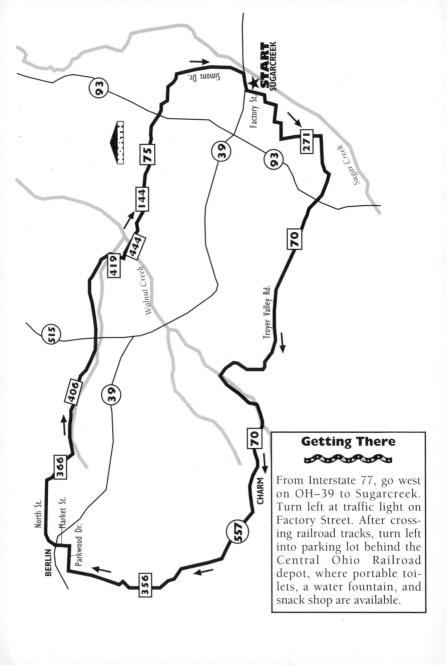

START
SUGARCREEK

Simons Dr.

Factory St.

93

93

271

75

144

444

419

515

406

39

366

North St.

Market St.

BERLIN

Parkwood Dr.

356

57

70

70

CHARM

39

Walnut Creek

Troyer Valley Rd.

Sugar Creek

NORTH

Getting There

From Interstate 77, go west on OH–39 to Sugarcreek. Turn left at traffic light on Factory Street. After crossing railroad tracks, turn left into parking lot behind the Central Ohio Railroad depot, where portable toilets, a water fountain, and snack shop are available.

DIREC-TIONS at a glance

0.0	Turn left (south) onto Factory Street.
0.1	Turn right at flashing red light onto Main Street.
0.1	Turn left at traffic signal onto Broadway.
0.4	Turn right onto Buckeye Street; stay on pavement.

0.7   Turn left onto Bahler Street.

1.1   Turn left onto Smokey Lane/Tuscarawas County 71.

1.9   Turn right to continue on Smokey Lane and enter Holmes County.

2.8   Turn right onto unpaved Seldenright Road.

3.4   Road becomes paved.

3.6   Cross OH–93 at stop sign. Road becomes Troyer Valley/CR 70.

7.0   Turn right to continue on CR 70 (remain on paved road).

8.0   Turn left to continue on CR 70.

10.9   Enter Charm.

11.0   Turn right at stop sign at T intersection on OH–557.

13.7   Turn right onto Township Road 356.

14.1   Road turns to gravel by transformer station.

14.4   Begin paved uphill stretch.

15.2   Turn right onto Parkwood Drive.

15.6   Turn left at stop sign onto Market Street.

16.0   Turn right onto North Street.

16.4   At stop sign, cross Bunker Hill Road/U.S. Highway 62 to continue on North Street/TR 366.

16.7   Road turns to gravel.

16.9   Cross TR 77 at stop sign to continue on TR 366.

17.4   Bear right to continue on TR 366, which is now paved but very rough.

18.6   Turn left at stop sign at T intersection onto TR 401.

18.7   Turn right onto unpaved TR 406 after crossing bridge.

19.7   Turn left at Y intersection to continue on TR 406.

21.9   Turn right onto unpaved TR 419.

22.4   Turn left at Y intersection onto unpaved TR 444.

22.9 Turn left at stop sign at **T** intersection onto CR 144.

23.9 Cross county line; road becomes CR 75.

25.1 Cross OH–93 at stop sign (caution: very bad sight lines) to continue on CR 75.

26.0 Turn right onto Simons Drive/TR 353.

26.7 Continue straight at stop sign onto Winklepleck Road.

27.2 Cautiously cross uneven railroad tracks.

27.4 Turn right at stop sign at **T** intersection on OH–39/Dover Road.

27.7 Turn left at traffic signal onto Factory Street.

28.0 Cross railroad tracks.

28.1 Turn left into railway depot parking lot to end ride.

---

for "English" cyclists. Holmes County is home to some of Ohio's most beautiful pastoral countryside. Its shops sell handmade goods such as furniture and quilts from true craftsmen.

Food is also big. One of the few vices of which the Amish partake is eating well. The restaurants in Amish country specialize in hearty country fare. It is often served home-style, with everyone taking helpings from bowls that never empty.

Your ride starts in Sugarcreek, a quaint Swiss town in far western Tuscarawas County. Downtown Sugarcreek was built to resemble an Alpine village. Its half-timbered buildings have window boxes overflowing with geraniums, and murals of mountains adorn the walls.

The route leaves Sugarcreek to the west and immediately enters Holmes County on its way to Charm, about 11 miles away. Charm is well-named, with its small collection of homes and shops. The ride leaves Charm to the north on OH–557. Enjoy this road surface; you will remember it fondly later. Outside of

Charm is the impressive Guggisberg Cheese Shop and Factory. Stop in and see baby Swiss cheese being made.

The tour now encounters the most challenging hills of the route. Take heart, for there are many places to rest and shop in Berlin, at Mile 15.9. Be careful, though, if you decide to explore along OH–39 in Berlin. It is very busy and an odd counterpoint to this otherwise placid countryside.

When you're sated with the plentiful craft and woodworking shops, remount your trusty steed and get ready for the most scenic roads on the tour. Many of the roads in the last 12 miles to Sugarcreek are lifted out of a lithograph from Currier and Ives, and they're also largely unpaved.

Relax and enjoy. You are riding where the tourist seldom goes: He is racing through on OH–39. You are riding the way of the local Amish boy going to Grandmother's house. Stop and pick a wildflower bouquet, then skip a stone in a stream. Life in the slow lane is not so bad.

WEIGHT
LIMIT
5
TONS

SPEED
LIMIT
25

Cross-State Challenge

Number of miles:	15.3 (21.2 longer option)
Approximate pedaling time:	2 hours (3 hours longer option)
Terrain:	Hilly
Traffic:	Moderately busy; West Virginia Highway 2 is generally busy
Things to see:	Old Fort Steuben, panoramic views in West Virginia and Pennsylvania
Facilities:	Food, water, and restrooms are available in Steubenville, Ohio, and Fallonsbee, West Virginia

How can this be a cross-state challenge when starting from Steubenville, Ohio is 230 miles across? The answer is that to the east, West Virginia is only 5 miles wide. Thus this ride starts in Ohio, crosses the entire state of West Virginia from west to east, hits Pennsylvania, and returns, and all before lunch.

Steubenville was founded on the site of Fort Steuben, the first U.S. military stronghold in the Northwest Territory. Old Fort Steuben, a replica of that first fort, is under construction. Several of the buildings are complete, and a neighboring park is planned for the near future. A gravel parking lot north of the re-created Old Fort Steuben is where the ride starts. Be sure to park right next to the fort rather than in the pay portion of the lot.

Downtown Steubenville is not at its best right now. It is a steel town still suffering through the transition from large, inefficient mills to smaller, more profitable ones. But amid the sadness of closed storefronts and lost dreams are pearls not to be missed. On walls all over town are murals, painted reminders of

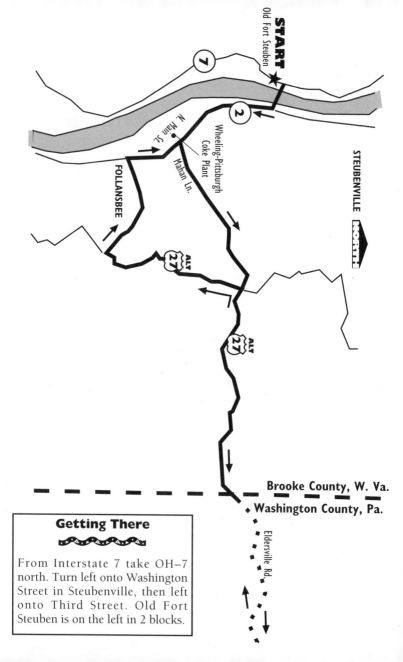

START
Old Fort Steuben

7

2

N. Main St.

Wheeling-Pittsburgh
Coke Plant

Mahan Ln.

FOLLANSBEE

STEUBENVILLE

NORTH

ALT
27

ALT
27

Brooke County, W. Va.
Washington County, Pa.

Eldersville Rd.

Getting There

From Interstate 7 take OH–7
north. Turn left onto Washington
Street in Steubenville, then left
onto Third Street. Old Fort
Steuben is on the left in 2 blocks.

DIREC-TIONS at a glance

0.0 Turn right onto Third Street out of Old Fort Steuben parking lot.

0.0 Turn right at light onto Market Street.

0.1 Take walkway on bridge's south side across Ohio River.

0.4 Turn right (south) onto West Virginia Route 2.

1.7 Turn left onto Mahan Lane at Howdy's Dairy Owl.

3.0 Begin steep two-stage climb.

3.8 Cross and continue east on alternate WV–27 at stop sign.

6.7 Turn around at intersection with State Line Road.

For long ride option see below.

9.5 Turn left to continue on alternate WV–27.

11.4 Turn right at stop sign to continue on alternate WV–27. Use caution, steep downhill.

12.8 Turn right at traffic light onto North Main Street/WV–2.

14.0 Wheeling–Pittsburgh Coke Plant is on the left.

14.8 Turn left at traffic light to cross bridge to Steubenville. Remember to take the walkway on the south side.

15.3 Turn left at traffic light onto Third Street.

15.3 Turn left into parking lot to end ride.

Long ride option, from State Line Road in West Virginia, to Eldersville, Pennsylvania.

6.7 Continue east on Eldersville Road from the West Virginia–Pennsylvania state line.

9.1 Turn right at Y intersection onto Cedar Grove Road in Eldersville.

9.6 Turn around at the Jefferson Township Garage on the left at edge of town and retrace your route on Cedar Grove Road.

10.2 Turn left at stop sign onto Eldersville Road. Follow the sign for Follansbee.

12.6 Enter Brooke County, West Virginia. The road surface changes and it becomes alternate WV–27. Pick up regular route description (Mile 9.5) to return to Steubenville.

Steubenville's bustling past and hopes for the future. While a tour of the murals is not included here, you might want to bike or walk around downtown and enjoy these treasures.

West Virginia is called the Mountaineer State for good reason. Across the Ohio River from Steubenville, sheer cliffs rise above the water. Fear not! There are ways up these hills that don't involve the use of climbing ropes and pitons. Still this climb out of the Ohio Valley is the most difficult in this book.

These parts of West Virginia and Pennsylvania have lots of unpaved roads. For road bikes, steep and unpaved shouldn't mix. This ride, therefore, is out and back on mostly the same roads. It is not overly steep, and the roads have good surfaces. Enjoy them; it took a while to find them.

The short version of this ride takes you out of the Ohio Valley and across West Virginia to the Pennsylvania state line, at Mile 6.7. The only clues that you are entering a new state will be a change in the road surface and a sign stating ENTERING WASHINGTON COUNTY. Pump your fists into the air, pat yourself on the back and turn around if conquering West Virginia is adventure enough for you. If you want to go to the first town in Pennsylvania, Eldersville is about 3 miles farther. There are no services there, but there are a number of nice vistas along the way.

Your climbing begins in earnest at Mile 3.0. The hill is steep, and in two stages. Once you reach the top, the terrain will be rolling but not so steep.

Use caution on the steep downhill at Mile 11.4 (short route) or Mile 17.3. Once you reach the bottom of this hill, there is no more climbing.

One last piece of advice: Take the walkway on the south side of the bridge when crossing the Ohio River. The bridge is narrow and has a metal-grate deck that is unstable to ride on and extremely slick in wet weather. You'll have to carry your bike up a flight of stairs to reach the walkway.

A Bicyclist's Bouquet

Number of miles:	9.9
Approximate pedaling time:	1.5 hours
Terrain:	Flat to moderately hilly
Traffic:	Mostly light except on OH–83
Things to see:	Lake Park Recreational Area, Roscoe Village, *Monticello III* canal boat ride
Facilities:	Picnic shelters, water, restrooms, playground, swimming, and camping in Lake Park; restaurants, stores, and an inn at Roscoe Village

Imagine yourself to be Colonel Henry Bouquet. It is 1764, and you've come to the Ohio Country to demand the release of captured white civilians. You would rather awe the Indians than fight them. So when you march through the thick woods with your army of 1,500 men, you send a team ahead to chop down trees so your boys can walk four abreast. The Indians were impressed, and they freed more than 200 captives.

Coshocton is the site of Bouquet's bloodless victory, and it is also the setting of a bouquet of flat roads and hills, town and country, forests and fields.

Start your ride in Coshocton County's Lake Park, where there is plenty of free parking, picnic facilities, water, and restrooms (at the swimming lake). There's even a campground along the Walhonding River, should you want to spend several days exploring east-central Ohio. As you leave the park on your ride, check out the historic roadside marker on the right to learn more about Bouquet's expedition.

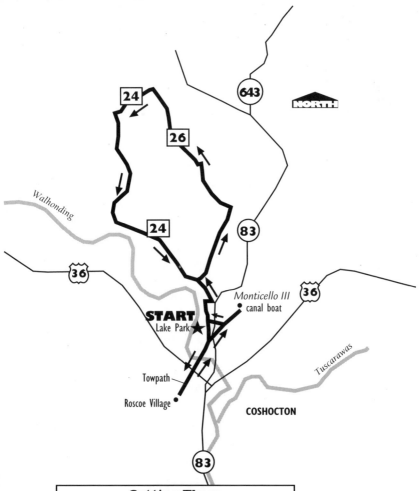

24
643
NORTH
26
Walhonding
24
83
36
Monticello III canal boat
36
START Lake Park
Tuscarawas
Towpath
Roscoe Village
COSHOCTON
83

Getting There

From Interstate 77, go west on U.S. Highway 36. Before reaching Coshocton, turn right onto OH–83 (follow signs to Lake Park). Turn left in to the park, drive straight back, then left in to the picnic parking area.

DIRECTIONS at a glance

0.0	Turn right out of picnic parking lot and head out the driveway of Lake Park.
0.1	Turn left at stop sign onto OH–83.
0.5	Turn left onto Coshocton County Road 24.
1.0	Turn right at Y intersection onto Township Road 26.

2.0 Turn left at Y intersection to continue on TR 26.

2.7 Jog left onto TR 28, then right to continue on TR 26.

3.9 Turn left at stop sign at Y intersection onto CR 24.

4.4 Turn left to continue on CR 24.

6.3 Road name becomes Riverview Avenue.

7.3 Turn right at Y intersection to remain on CR 24.

7.7 Turn right at stop sign at T intersection onto OH–83.

8.2 Turn right into Lake Park, then immediately left and right onto asphalt path. This is the towpath to Roscoe Village.

9.0 Get off towpath at Roscoe Village visitors center. To return to Lake Park, go back on towpath.

9.7 To go to *Monticello III* canal boat, turn right after crossing river. To leave canal boat, return to this point and turn right.

9.8 Turn left off towpath and go down a short hill into the park.

9.9 End ride in picnic area parking lot.

The traffic on OH–83 just outside the park is moderately heavy, but take heart; the route quickly takes you onto county and township roads. You will wind through farmers' fields and over wooded hills. In summer the overwhelming impression is of the color green in the fields and on the hills.

Another historic marker about Bouquet marks your 1 mile point, on the left at the Y intersection where you turn right onto Township Road 26. After this point you'll also encounter some hills. Note that the downhills at miles 3 and 5 are steep, and the second hill is curvy as well. When County Road 24 becomes Riverview Avenue you can rest easy, for the terrain will flatten out for the remainder of the ride.

When you return to Lake Park, get on the asphalt path that will take you .8 mile along the old towpath to Roscoe Village, a restored nineteenth-century canal town. Here you can shop in a variety of specialty stores, choose among five restaurants, or take a living history tour that includes costumed craftsmen and interpreters demonstrating old-time crafts. The Johnson–Humrickhouse Museum has collections of American Indian artifacts, early American artifacts, oriental antiquities, and nineteenth- and twentieth-century American and European decorative art. The village holds weekend theme festivals throughout the year, too.

On your way back to Lake Park on the pleasant shady towpath, turn to the right after crossing the river to take a 1.5-mile trip on the *Monticello III,* a replica 1800s canal boat. The tours on the restored section of the Ohio & Erie Canal depart hourly from 1:00 to 5:00 P.M. daily from Memorial Day through Labor Day and on weekends from Labor Day to mid-October.

Cinnamon Bun Delight

Number of miles:	31
Approximate pedaling time:	3.5 hours
Terrain:	Flat to gently rolling
Traffic:	Generally light, except on federal and state highways
Things to see:	Amish restaurants, Little Darby Covered Bridge, Smith Cemetery State Nature Preserve, Bigelow Pioneer Cemetery State Nature Preserve
Facilities:	Food, drink, and restrooms are available in the Amish restaurants on U.S. Highway 42; Country Corners carryout store in Resaca; and the Evans Carryout in Unionville Center

This is a ride for the cyclist who rides to eat and eats to ride. Columbus-area bicyclists ride to Plain City on Saturday mornings just to partake of the generously portioned meals at the Dutch Kitchen and Der Dutchman restaurants. Both are Amish/Mennonite eateries that feature simple, tasty, and bountiful meals. Of special note is the breakfast at the Dutch Kitchen, where the delicious cinnamon buns are practically a meal in themselves.

The hungriest of cyclists might choose to begin this ride with a bite at one restaurant and end with a meal at the other one. Just remember, the restaurants are closed on Sundays.

Start your ride at Der Dutchman Restaurant, because it is larger than the Dutch Kitchen, just 2.6 miles down U.S. High-

way 42, and has a large parking lot. Be courteous to the regular customers and park in the very back of the lot.

This mostly flat region just northeast of Columbus was known as the Darby Plains when the first white settlers arrived in the early 1800s, and the landscape was far different from what you see now. Prairie grasses grew 8 to 10 feet tall in dense sod, making the clearing, draining, plowing, and planting of the land back-breaking labor. Pioneers, however, persisted. The prairie grasses—big bluestem, little bluestem, cord grass and Indian grass—gave way to corn. The land that wasn't farmed was used as pasture for the farmers' livestock.

Soon the wild prairie was reduced to scattered remnants, mostly along roadsides, fence rows, and railroad tracks. Modern farming practices and herbicides virtually destroyed even these remnants, except in two cemeteries. The last resting place of the brave, hard-working settlers also became the last refuge of the prairie.

Today, Bigelow Cemetery, at Mile 16.3, and Smith Cemetery, at Mile 27.6, are state nature preserves. These small, easy-to-overlook parcels of land have never been plowed or grazed, and the wildflowers and grasses provide color from midsummer through fall. The peak of summer color is late July through August, with waist-high flowers of yellow, red, purple, and lavender. In fall, clumps of grass 6 to 8 feet tall dapple the land with red-gold and orange.

Be sure to take a close look at the gravestones tucked among the prairie grasses. They mutely tell of great sorrow: a child who didn't survive infancy here, a mother who died in childbirth there, and whole families that succumbed to epidemics. At the same time, some markers tell triumphant tales, as some hardy individuals survived into their 80s in an era when the average life span rarely exceeded 50 years.

You'll cross the 1873 Little Darby Covered Bridge about a mile after the Bigelow Cemetery. Then it's on to the village of Unionville Center at Mile 24.3, where food and drink are available at Evans Carryout. Don't succumb to your hunger pangs

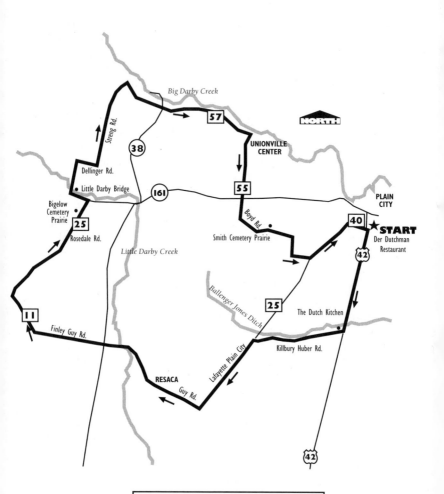

Big Darby Creek

NORTH

57

Streng Rd.

UNIONVILLE
CENTER

38

Dellinger Rd.

• Little Darby Bridge

161

55

Bigelow
Cemetery
Prairie

Boyd Rd. •

PLAIN
CITY

25

Rosedale Rd.

Smith Cemetery Prairie

40

★ **START**
Der Dutchman
Restaurant

42

Little Darby Creek

Ballenger Jones Ditch

25

The Dutch Kitchen

11

Finley Guy Rd.

Lafayette Plain City

Killbury Huber Rd.

RESACA
Guy Rd.

42

Getting There

From Interstate 70, go north ap-
proximately 12 miles on U.S. Highway 42 until you see Der
Dutchman Restaurant on the right.

DIRECTIONS at a glance

0.0 Leave Der Dutchman Restaurant and turn left on U.S. Highway 42.

2.6 Dutch Kitchen Restaurant is on the right.

2.8 Turn right onto Killbury Huber Road, and pass Jonathan Alder High School.

5.1 Turn left onto Lafayette–Plain City Road/Madison County Road 5.

7.4 Turn right onto Finley Guy Road.

9.0 Go through Resaca.

9.8 Turn left at Y intersection to continue on Finley Guy Road.

10.5 Cross OH–38 at stop sign.

12.3 Turn right on Rosedale–Milford Center Road/CR 11.

13.4 At stop sign, turn right on Rosedale Road/CR 25.

16.3 Bigelow Cemetery Prairie State Nature Preserve is on the left (look for overgrown area).

16.6 Turn left at stop sign at T intersection onto OH–161.

17.0 Turn right onto Axe Handle Road/Union County 82.

17.1 Cross Little Darby Covered Bridge.

18.0 Turn right onto Dellinger Road/Township Road 66.

18.5 Turn left at stop sign at T intersection onto Streng Road/TR 67.

20.8 Turn right onto Middleburg–Plain City Road/CR 57.

22.0 Cross OH–38 at stop sign.

24.5 Turn right onto Unionville Road/CR55, and pass an old schoolhouse on the right.

26.1 Cautiously cross OH–161 at stop sign. Road becomes North Boyd south of OH–161.

26.6 Turn left at stop sign at T intersection onto Boyd Road/Madison County 42.

27.6 Smith Cemetery Prairie State Nature Preserve is on left.

28.1 Turn right at stop sign at T intersection on Converse Chapel Road/CR 41.

28.6 Turn left at stop sign at T intersection on Converse Huff Road/CR 30.

29.1 Turn left at stop sign on Lafayette–Plain City Road/CR 5.
30.4 Turn right onto Perry Pike/CR 40.
31.0 Cross U.S. Highway 42/Jefferson Avenue at stop sign, and enter Der Dutchman Restaurant parking lot to end ride.

---

just yet, for the end of your ride and Der Dutchman Restaurant are only an easy 7 miles away!

Although the terrain is gentle on this ride, wind may be a factor. That is why the suggested route is clockwise: Fight the wind first, while your legs are fresh, then return with the following breeze.

Out of Africa

Number of miles:	23.9
Approximate pedaling time:	2.5 hours
Terrain:	Flat to gently rolling
Traffic:	Can be heavy in Powell and near the Columbus Zoo and Wyandot Lake
Things to see:	Alum Creek State Park, antique shopping in Powell; Columbus Zoo, Wyandot Lake Adventure Park
Facilities:	Restaurants and stores in Powell and the Columbus Zoo; picnic facilities, water, and restrooms at Alum Creek State Park, the Columbus Zoo and Wyandot Lake; bike racks at the Columbus Zoo; camping, beach, and mountain-bike trails at Alum Creek State Park

Africa, a mere crossroads minutes from Columbus and seconds from our starting point, lends its name to this ride because the destination is the Columbus Zoo. This zoo has a large collection of African animals, including lions, black rhinos, zebras, and marabou storks. Animals are not the only significant element to this ride; human history plays a role as well.

Before the late 1850s, the crossroads called Africa was a hamlet named East Orange. There was a cluster of small cabins there built to serve as temporary housing while their owners built permanent homes in Westerville.

In 1859, a slave owner in North Carolina died, and his

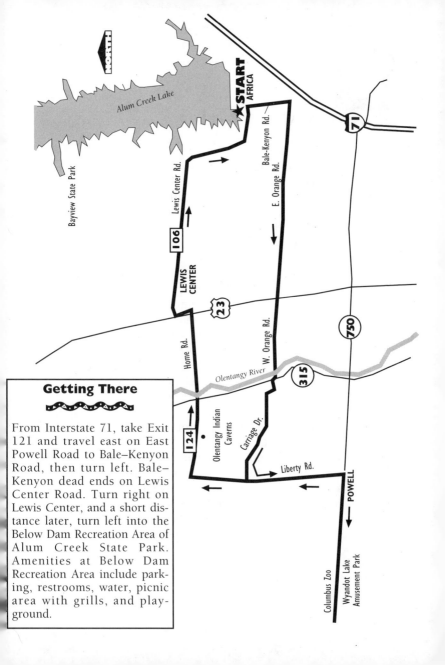

NORTH

Alum Creek Lake

★ START
AFRICA

Bayview State Park

Lewis Center Rd.

Bale–Kenyon Rd.

E. Orange Rd.

106

LEWIS CENTER

71

23

750

Home Rd.

W. Orange Rd.

Olentangy River

315

Getting There

From Interstate 71, take Exit 121 and travel east on East Powell Road to Bale–Kenyon Road, then turn left. Bale–Kenyon dead ends on Lewis Center Road. Turn right on Lewis Center, and a short distance later, turn left into the Below Dam Recreation Area of Alum Creek State Park. Amenities at Below Dam Recreation Area include parking, restrooms, water, picnic area with grills, and playground.

124

Olentangy Indian Caverns

Carriage Dr.

Liberty Rd.

POWELL

Columbus Zoo

Wyandot Lake Amusement Park

DIRECTIONS at a glance

0.0   To leave Below Dam Recreation Area parking lot, turn right at stop sign onto Lewis Center Road/County Road 106.

0.1   Turn left onto Bale–Kenyon Road.

0.8   Turn right onto East Orange Road/Township Road 114.

2.4   Cross Old State Road at stop sign.

3.3   Cross two sets of railroad tracks.

4.0   Cross OH–23 at traffic signal. Caution: busy four-lane highway with high-speed traffic.

5.2   Cross Olentangy River on one-lane bridge.

5.3   Jog right at stop sign onto OH–315, then left onto Carriage Drive/TR 334.

7.1   Turn left at stop sign onto Liberty Road.

8.8   Turn right at stop sign onto OH–750/Powell Road.

8.9   Cross triple-set railroad tracks.

11.2   Turn left at stop sign onto OH–257/Riverside Drive.

11.5   Turn left into Columbus Zoo/Wyandot Lake parking lot. To leave the zoo or amusement park, come back out this entrance and turn right onto OH–257/Riverside Drive.

11.8   Turn right onto OH–750/Powell Road.

14.0   Cross three sets of railroad tracks.

14.1   Turn left at stop sign onto Liberty Road out of Powell.

16.7   Turn right at stop sign at T intersection on Home Road/County Road 124.

17.4   Turn right to visit Olentangy Indian Caverns. To leave the caverns turn right onto Home Road.

17.9   Cautiously cross busy OH–315 at stop sign.

18.0   Cross Olentangy River on one-lane bridge.

19.3   Turn left at traffic light onto OH–23.

19.6   Turn right at traffic light onto Lewis Center Road/CR 106.

20.6   Cross rough double set railroad tracks.

21.6   Cross Old State Road at stop sign.

22.4   Alum Creek State Park Beach is on left.

22.8 Alum Creek State Park Visitors Center is on left.
23.9 Turn left into Below Dam Recreation Area to end ride.

widow freed the family's slaves. The group of thirty-five freed slaves made their way north and across the Ohio River. The group reached Westerville, which was strongly anti-slavery. Here the freed slaves were accepted and taken to the cabins north of town and invited to settle. They were offered jobs helping local farmers with the harvesting.

So the freed slaves settled in the cabins and became active in the Underground Railroad. They helped feed, shelter, and guide escaping slaves, risking fines, imprisonment, and potential kidnapping and return to slavery in the South. One even joined the Union Army and fought in the Civil War.

One of the few pro-slavery landowners in the area sarcastically referred to the community of escaped slaves as Africa, and the name stuck. Although the cabins in the woods and the few homes, businesses, and church that made up Africa are mostly gone, the name lives on in the crossroads and the name of the road just east of Alum Creek State Park.

The starting point is virtually in the shadow of the Alum Creek Lake dam, in the Below Dam Recreation Area in the state park. From here the ride rolls through a combination of outer Columbus suburbs and woods.

Powell, about 8.5 miles into the ride, is a busy little town teeming with antiques shops. The zoo is at Mile 11.5, along with Wyandot Lake Adventure Park, which has an amusement park plus an impressive collection of water slides to enjoy on hot summer days.

Another way to cool off on a hot day is to stop for a tour of Olentangy Indian Caverns, at Mile 17.4. The temperature inside the caverns is a steady fifty-four degrees Fahrenheit.

Your final chance to cool off is at Alum Creek State Park Beach, Ohio's largest inland beach. The turn-off is on the left at Mile 22.4, just 1.5 miles from the end of the ride.

Be careful because traffic is heavy on U.S. Highway 23 and Ohio highways 315, 750, and 257. Use caution when crossing or riding these roads. Every attempt has been made to cross these roads only at traffic signals and to minimize the distances rode on them. When riding on these roads, use the generally wide paved shoulders.

Teutonic Village Volksbike

Number of miles:	4.0 miles
Approximate pedaling time:	30 minutes
Terrain:	Flat
Surface:	Brick streets
Traffic:	Urban but not main thoroughfares
Things to see:	German Village
Facilities:	Food is readily available; public restrooms and water at Schiller Park and Recreation Center

Just south of downtown Columbus is one square mile of once-blighted inner city. In 1959 a movement started to renovate the solid brick houses that many persons believed needed the wrecking ball. In the intervening forty years, more than 1,600 buildings have had their old-world charm restored.

Today German Village is a fascinating collection of charming nineteenth-century brick homes, shops, galleries, and restaurants. Some are grand, many are unpretentious, and all are lovingly kept. It is a feast for both the eyes and palate, because German Village contains many of Columbus's trendiest dining spots.

In 1814 the area was known as South Columbus and you had to walk some distance to get into town. Then German immigrants started moving into the neighborhood. They were tradesmen, stonemasons, brewers, and farmers. They built a community that looked very much like their homes in the fatherland; brick-solid, with enough ornamentation to keep the frau happy.

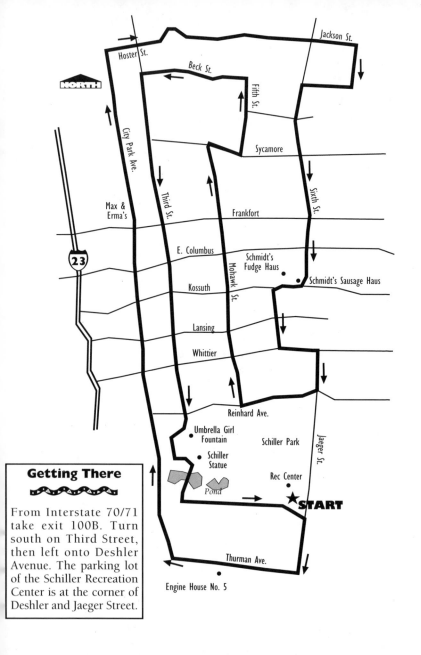

Jackson St.

Hoster St.

Beck St.

Fifth St.

NORTH

City Park Ave.

Sycamore

Third St.

Sixth St.

Max & Erma's

Frankfort

23

E. Columbus

Schmidt's Fudge Haus

Schmidt's Sausage Haus

Mohawk St.

Kossuth

Lansing

Whittier

Reinhard Ave.

Umbrella Girl Fountain

Schiller Park

Jaeger St.

Schiller Statue

Rec Center

Pond

★ START

Getting There

From Interstate 70/71 take exit 100B. Turn south on Third Street, then left onto Deshler Avenue. The parking lot of the Schiller Recreation Center is at the corner of Deshler and Jaeger Street.

Thurman Ave.

Engine House No. 5

DIRECTIONS at a glance

0.0	Turn right from Schiller Recreation Center parking lot onto Jaeger Street.
0.1	Turn right at traffic light onto Thurman Avenue.
0.2	Turn right onto City Park Avenue.
1.0	Turn right onto Hoster Street.

1.1 Cross Third Street at traffic light. (Thun's Backerei and Katzinger's are one block to left.)

1.1 Turn left at stop sign onto Lazelle Street.

1.1 Turn right at stop sign onto Jackson Street.

1.4 Turn right at stop sign onto Grant Avenue.

1.5 Turn right at stop sign onto Beck Street.

1.6 Turn left onto Sixth Street.

1.7 At stop sign, jog left, then right, across Sycamore Street to continue on Sixth Street.

1.9 Turn right at stop sign onto Kossuth Street.

2.0 Turn left onto Fifth Street.

2.1 Turn left at stop sign at T intersection onto Whittier Street.

2.2 Turn right at light onto Jaeger Street.

2.3 Turn right onto Reinhard Avenue.

2.4 Turn right onto Mohawk Street.

2.7 Turn right onto Sycamore Street.

2.8 Turn left onto Fifth Street.

2.9 Turn left at stop sign onto Beck Street.

3.0 Turn left at stop sign onto Third Street.

3.6 Cross Reinhard Street at stop sign to enter park.

3.6 Turn right onto asphalt path and pass behind Umbrella Girl fountain.

3.7 Turn left and go down aisle of flowers to Schiller statue.

3.7 Turn right onto asphalt path to cross pond.

3.8 Turn left at T intersection to pass behind the pond.

4.0 Enter recreation center parking lot to end ride.

Some residents were prosperous, but most were solidly middle class. They built two churches: Trinity Lutheran and St. Mary's Roman Catholic. They built a Lutheran theological seminary, which later became Capital University. The schools their children attended used German-language books.

Then came World War I, and with it, rampant anti-German sentiment. German-language education stopped; everyone spoke only English to show how American they were. Later, Prohibition closed the breweries, which were major employers. These two events culturally and economically devastated the area.

The sturdy hard-working people drifted away to newer English-speaking neighborhoods. By the 1950s the village was a slum. Many properties were vacant, and the area was slated for urban renewal.

In 1960 the German Village Society was founded. Its 183 charter members worked tirelessly with government officials, property owners, and investors against enormous odds. Their success is this beautiful gentrified little piece of urban magic. German Village is the largest privately funded restoration of its kind in the United States. It is a model others strive to duplicate.

Most people tour the village by car, but many walk, and this tour explains how to tour it by bike. Be prepared for narrow brick streets. Also bring along a lock, so you can enjoy the stops along the way.

Start and end at Schiller Park, twenty-three acres of playgrounds, athletic fields, flower gardens, and ponds. The park's recreation center has restrooms and water fountains.

German Village is home to many galleries that display everything from glass to floral creations. Around every corner is an interesting shop to discover. There are also many bed-and-breakfast inns, if you want to prolong your lederhosen adventure.

Most important to the hungry cyclist are the many restaurants. Among them are Engine House No. 5 (Mile 0.1), Katzinger's Deli (a block off the route at Mile 1.1), Schmidt's Sausage Haus (Mile 1.9), and the first Max & Erma's (Mile 3.2). There are also cafes, bakeries, ice cream shops, and Schmidt's candy shop.

Ohio's Interstate 1

Number of miles:	23.4
Approximate pedaling time:	2.5 hours
Terrain:	Gently rolling, with a few bigger hills
Traffic:	Generally light, except on state and federal routes
Things to see:	Remnants of Ohio's canal era; 1900 Rock Mill Covered Bridge and 1888 Hartman Covered Bridge; restored antique gas station
Facilities:	Restaurants and stores in Canal Winchester and Lithopolis; picnic site with water, shelter, and portable toilet at Lockville Park

Ohio's first "interstate highway" system was begun in 1825. It was more than 800 miles long, but the speed limit was only 4 m.p.h.—a limit you will easily, and lawfully, exceed—as you ride along.

The first highway in this system was the 309-mile Ohio & Erie Canal. It stretched from Cleveland on Lake Erie to Portsmouth on the Ohio River and climbed up and down a total of 1,206 feet through 156 locks. This marvel of engineering took a little over seven years to construct.

Once the canal was completed, Ohio farmers had access to the Eastern markets and made decent money for their crops. While Ohio's agricultural bounty flowed out of the state, settlers and merchandise poured in. In addition to agriculture, industry also boomed. Much-needed money arrived, stabilizing the econ-

omy and bolstering Ohioans' confidence.

Unfortunately, the heyday of the canals was short-lived. Railroads came to Ohio only a few short years after the 1832 completion of the Ohio & Erie Canal. In the 1850s the railroads started cutting sharply into the canals' business. The canals limped along, though, mainly transporting bulk goods such as coal, lumber, sand, and gravel that were not economical to ship by train.

The death knell of Ohio's canal system was dealt by Mother Nature in one fell swoop. In March 1913, every river in the state flooded, wiping out what remained of the canal network. Now scattered ditches and lock ruins are all that remain of this important era of Ohio history.

This ride explores an area of south-central Ohio that was dominated by the Ohio & Erie canal. Canal Winchester, your starting point, was 210 miles by canal from Lake Erie. Lockville was 206 miles by canal from the lake. Walnut Creek, which you'll cross, was the water source for the canal in this area. As you cycle through the undulating farmland, keep your eyes open for the tree lines, shallow ditches, and stone walls that signal the remnants of Ohio's first interstate.

Lockville Park, at Mile 5.1, is a great picnic site. Be sure to explore the lock ruins and the 1888 Hartman Covered Bridge and read the signs to get a good feel for the canal era.

After Lockville Park the terrain is hillier. Your reward for climbing a longish hill at Mile 7.6 is a great view, especially to the north. Be careful when descending, though, because your turn onto Coonpath Road is easy to miss if you're going too fast. Coonpath Road is another road to exercise control on, because you must stop and turn right in the middle of a steep downhill at Mile 10.

The village of Lithopolis is the hometown of A.W. Wagnall, who with Isaac K. Funk produced Funk & Wagnalls Standard Dictionary of the English Language in 1893. At Mile 20.1, you'll pass the Wagnall Memorial Library. From here it is an easy 3-mile ride back to Canal Winchester.

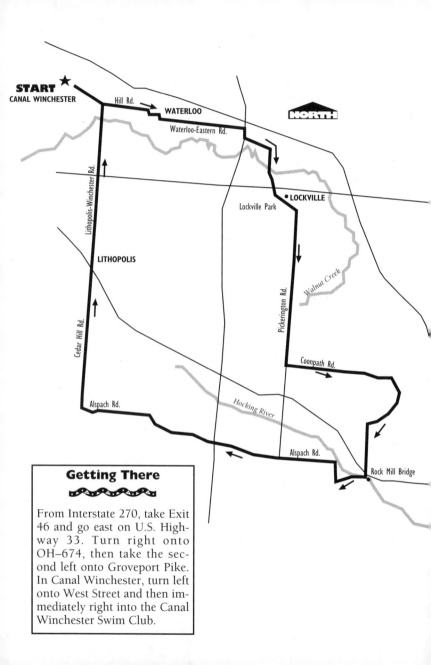

START
CANAL WINCHESTER

Hill Rd.

WATERLOO

Waterloo-Eastern Rd.

NORTH

Lithopolis-Winchester Rd.

Lockville Park

● **LOCKVILLE**

LITHOPOLIS

Pickerington Rd.

Walnut Creek

Cedar Hill Rd.

Coonpath Rd.

Alspach Rd.

Hocking River

Alspach Rd.

Rock Mill Bridge

Getting There

From Interstate 270, take Exit 46 and go east on U.S. Highway 33. Turn right onto OH–674, then take the second left onto Groveport Pike. In Canal Winchester, turn left onto West Street and then immediately right into the Canal Winchester Swim Club.

DIREC-TIONS at a glance

0.0 Begin in the parking lot of the Canal Winchester Swim Club. Turn right onto West Street.

0.1 Turn right at stop sign onto West Waterloo Road, which eventually becomes Hill Road after leaving town.

1.6 Turn right at T intersection onto Waterloo Eastern Road.

1.7 Turn right at T intersection onto Diley Road. Road takes a ninety-degree left turn and becomes Waterloo Eastern again.

3.5 Turn right at T intersection onto Amanda Northern Road.

3.6 Turn left onto Benadum Road.

4.1 Turn right at T intersection onto Pickerington Road.

5.2 Turn right into Lockville Park. To leave park, continue out parking lot.

5.3 Turn right from parking lot onto Pickerington Road.

6.7 Look left just before a small hill to see a restored antique gas station and old cars.

8.1 Turn left onto Coonpath Road at bottom of hill.

10.0 Turn right at stop sign onto Carroll Southern Road.

10.3 Turn right onto Lamb Road.

11.9 Cross busy Lithopolis Road at stop sign to cross Rock Mill Covered Bridge (road becomes Rock Mill Road after crossing Lithopolis).

12.5 Turn right onto Alspach Road and begin a gradual climb.

17.5 Turn right onto Cedar Hill Road.

19.9 Turn left at stop sign onto East Columbus Street.

20.1 Turn right onto Walnut Street, which quickly becomes Lithopolis–Winchester Road. Pass Wagnall Memorial Library on right.

22.4 Continue into Canal Winchester, where road becomes East Columbus Street.

23.0 After stop sign, continue straight onto West Columbus Street.

23.1 Turn right at flasher onto Washington Road.

23.2 Turn left onto Groveport Pike.
23.4 Turn right onto West Street.
23.4 Turn right into Canal Winchester Swim Club parking lot.

A Scoop of Licking County

Number of miles:	17.7
Approximate pedaling time:	2.5 hours
Terrain:	Moderately hilly
Surface:	A few stretches of gravel on Cooksey Road
Traffic:	Light, except on federal and state routes, particularly on weekends
Things to see:	Rolling green countryside, villages of St. Louisville and Utica, Velvet Ice Cream plant and Ye Olde Mill
Facilities:	Restaurants and stores in St. Louisville and Utica; food, water, restrooms and picnic shelters at Ye Olde Mill

Here's a taste of Licking County dedicated to the cyclist who believes a bike ride without ice cream is not much of a ride.

This sweet ride includes a rainbow of the features cyclists like most. Quiet villages give way to green-carpeted hills. Farmers' fields and groves of hardwood trees alternate on the hills and in the valleys. The peaceful roads range from newly paved to unpaved, although the latter total less than 1 mile. Best of all, this ride includes a stop at Ye Olde Mill, the home of Velvet Ice Cream.

The trip begins in the village of St. Louisville, at Community Park. After less than .5 mile, the countryside takes on a distinctly rural look.

The ascent into the hills begins 1.5 miles into the ride. After

a short, but steep, climb on Dog Leg Road, you will turn left onto Peat Moss Road/County Road 206 at Mile 1.9. Peat Moss Road is wonderful. Freshly paved in 1997, it offers beautiful views of farms nestled in the bright-green hills.

At Mile 4.4, on Cooksey Road, the asphalt peters out. Don't be discouraged, though; although the asphalt and gravel alternate several times, the gravel stretches are no longer than .3 mile each. Once you continue on Bell Church Road/Township Road 37 at Mile 5.7, there will be no more rocky roads.

At Mile 6.1, you'll cross the busy U.S. Highway 62/Millersburg Road and the Knox County line. Then you'll enjoy a mile-long coast downhill into the village of Utica.

After a few jogs on quiet residential streets in Utica, you'll emerge onto OH–13 for the last leg to Ye Olde Mill. This is a busy stretch, particularly on weekends when the mill is open from May 1 to November, so stay alert.

After nearly 2 miles on OH–13, the Velvet Ice Cream Company's showplace park offers a "Cherry Cordial" welcome at Mile 9.5. The current mill is the fourth built on the site of an 1817 grist mill that was one of the biggest in the Ohio frontier. It has an 18-foot wheel that still creaks and bumps as water pours over it, although it no longer turns a stone. The beautiful park around the mill includes ponds, picnic shelters, and playground equipment. Free entertainment is provided every weekend.

Inside there is a small ice cream and milling museum; a viewing gallery, where you might catch a glimpse of ice cream being made; a gift shop; and, of course, a restaurant and ice cream parlor. The latter serves homemade baked goods, sandwiches, salads, soups and more than thirty-one flavors of ice cream, frozen yogurt, and sherbet.

After resting your legs and satisfying any ice cream cravings you might have, head back north toward Utica on OH–13. Rather than go into town again, turn right onto Blacksnake Road/County Road 200 just before you reach U.S. Highway 62. The hustle and bustle of OH–13 will soon be a memory.

Although you must once again ride uphill to Peat Moss

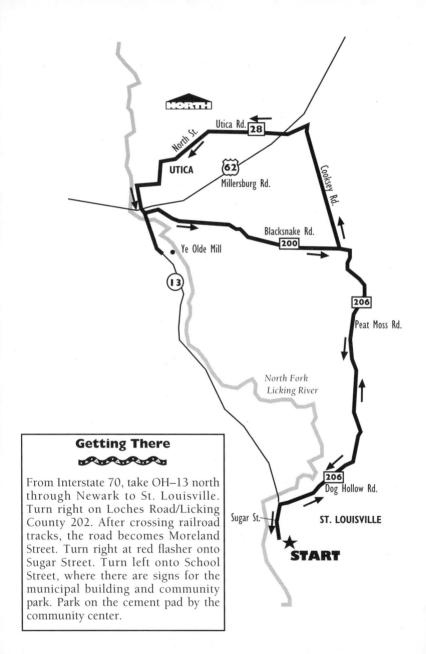

NORTH

Utica Rd. 28

North St.

UTICA

62

Millersburg Rd.

Cooksey Rd.

Blacksnake Rd.

200

Ye Olde Mill

13

206

Peat Moss Rd.

North Fork
Licking River

206

Dog Hollow Rd.

Sugar St.

ST. LOUISVILLE

START

Getting There

From Interstate 70, take OH–13 north through Newark to St. Louisville. Turn right on Loches Road/Licking County 202. After crossing railroad tracks, the road becomes Moreland Street. Turn right at red flasher onto Sugar Street. Turn left onto School Street, where there are signs for the municipal building and community park. Park on the cement pad by the community center.

DIREC-TIONS at a glance

0.0 Leave park by going back out School Street.
0.0 Turn right onto Sugar Street.
0.1 Cross Moreland Street.
0.4 Turn right at stop sign at T intersection onto Dog Hollow Road/Licking County 206.
1.9 Turn left onto Peat Moss Road/CR 206 at top of hill.
4.2 Turn left onto Blacksnake Road/CR 200.
4.3 Turn right onto Cooksey Road.
5.7 Continue straight onto Bell Church Road/Township Road 37 where it joins Cooksey from the right.
5.8 Take sharp left onto Utica Road/CR 28.
6.1 Carefully cross busy U.S. 62/Millersburg Road at stop sign to continue on Utica Road into town where it becomes North Street.
7.3 Turn left onto Jefferson Street.
7.7 Turn right at stop sign onto Spring Street.
7.8 Cross railroad tracks.
7.9 Turn left onto Main Street–OH–13 at traffic signal.
8.3 Cross U.S. Highway 62 at traffic signal to continue on OH–13.
9.5 Turn left into Ye Olde Mill. This is the third driveway in to the Velvet Ice Cream complex. To leave mill, go back out driveway and turn right onto OH–13.
10.6 Turn right onto Blacksnake Road/CR 200 immediately before U.S. Highway 62.
11.1 Cross rough railroad tracks that have no warning flashers.
13.4 Turn right on Peat Moss Road/CR 206.
15.7 Turn right at stop sign at T intersection onto Dog Hollow Road/CR 206.
17.1 Turn left onto Sugar Road.
17.6 Turn left onto School Street.
17.7 Enter Community Park/Municipal Building driveway to end ride.

Road, the climb is much more gentle from this side. And once you reach Peat Moss Road, the view of the surrounding valley is just as beautiful as it was the first time. Revel again in the smoothness of the road and the soothing green of the countryside, then enjoy the nice downhill run on Dog Leg Road that marks your final 2 miles into St. Louisville.

Seal of Approval Ride

Number of miles:	17.8
Approximate pedaling time:	2 hours
Terrain:	Rolling hills
Traffic:	Generally light except on state routes
Things to see:	Great Seal State Park and the setting that inspired the Great Seal of the State of Ohio
Facilities:	Picnic grounds, vault toilets, and primitive camping in Great Seal State Park; restaurants and stores in Kingston, on the route, and in Chillicothe, 5 miles from the ride's start

This south-central Ohio ride is sure to receive the cyclist's seal of approval, because it offers rolling, although not-too-steep, terrain with some nice views of the Appalachian foothills. The ride is largely rural in nature despite starting just a few minutes off a heavily traveled state highway corridor.

Chillicothe, about 5 miles south of the starting point in Great Seal State Park, became the first capital of the Northwest Territory in 1800. A few years later it was named the first capital of the state of Ohio.

The beauty of the hills to the east appealed to William Creighton, an early Ohio secretary of state who was given the task of designing a state seal. One evening he and several other guests visited the home of Thomas Worthington, one of the state's founders, in the countryside near Chillicothe. The men

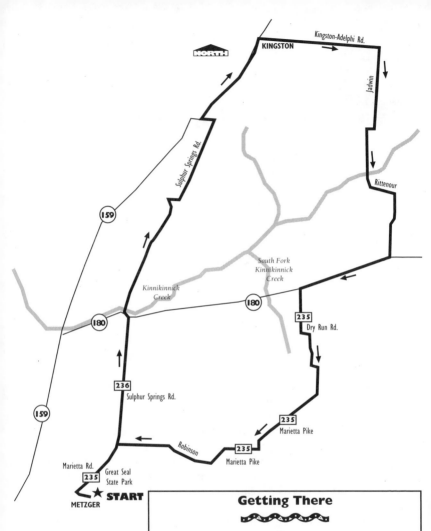

NORTH

KINGSTON

Kingston-Adelphi Rd.

Jadwin

Rittenour

Sulphur Springs Rd.

159

South Fork
Kinnikinnick
Creek

Kinnikinnick
Creek

180

235
Dry Run Rd.

180

236
Sulphur Springs Rd.

235
Marietta Pike

159

Robinson

235
Marietta Pike

Marietta Rd.

235 Great Seal
State Park

★ **START**

METZGER

Getting There

From Interstate 71 go south on U.S. Highway 35. Exit onto North Business Loop 23. Two miles later, turn right onto Hopetown Road (after the Gaslite Inn) and go immediately under a railroad overpass. After a mile pass an A-frame house as the road changes its name to Marietta Road. Go through Metzger Village, then turn right into Great Seal State Park and drive straight back to the picnic area.

0.0   Leave Great Seal State Park's picnic area parking lot.

0.5   Turn right at stop sign onto Marietta Road/Ross County 235.

1.1   Cross Delano Road at stop sign to continue on Sulphur Springs Road/CR 236.

2.7   Jog left onto OH–180 at stop sign at Y intersection, then right, to remain on Sulphur Springs.

4.2   Jog right onto Snyder Road at T intersection, to remain on Sulphur Springs.

5.5   Rest area with restroom and picnic area is on left at stop sign. To leave rest area, turn right at stop sign onto OH–159. OH–159 becomes Main Street in Kingston.

6.7   Turn right onto Kingston–Adelphi Road/County Line Road.

8.2   Turn right onto Jadwin Road.

9.2   Turn right at stop sign at T intersection onto Kingston–Hickle Road/TH 279.

9.3   Turn left onto Rittenour Road/TH 249–B.

11.1 Turn right at stop sign at T intersection on OH–180.

12.3 Turn left onto Dry Run Road/CR 223.

13.7 Turn right at Y intersection onto Marietta Pike/CR 235.

14.7 Turn right to remain on Marietta Pike.

15.1 Turn left onto Robinson Road/TH 220.

15.3 Turn right at Y intersection to remain on Robinson.

16.5 Turn left at stop sign onto Marietta Road/CR 235.

17.2 Turn left into Great Seal State Park.

17.8 End ride at picnic area parking lot.

spent the evening conversing and playing cards. At dawn the next day, they walked across Worthington's estate and saw the sun rising behind Mount Logan. Legend has it that Creighton was impressed with the view and said, "Gentlemen, there is our state seal."

Creighton drew up the state seal showing the sun rising over mountains, because Ohio was the first state west of the Alleghenies. A field of wheat is in the foreground, with a sheaf of wheat symbolizing Ohio the bountiful and a sheaf of seventeen arrows symbolizing Ohio's status as the seventeenth state. Great Seal State Park was established in 1980 to protect the setting that inspired the state seal and to honor the wilderness spirit of early Ohio.

The ride starts with a descent from the state park picnic area to Marietta Road. At Mile 2.7, you'll pass Zane Trace High School, which is named after one of the five major Indian trails that intersected in this area.

A tiny roadside rest area welcomes tired travelers at the intersection of Sulphur Springs Road and Highway 159. Kingston, shortly after the rest stop, offers a chance to buy food. Just north of town, Kingston–Adelphi Road/County Line Road is the northernmost point of the ride.

This ride is notable mostly for its quiet natural beauty, but Mile 9.5 brings a manmade landmark; a statue of a rearing horse. Continue pedaling up hill and down, between farmer's fields and with the Appalachian ridge always to the east. When you pass some suburban housing developments, you'll know your journey is nearly over.

It is interesting to try to spy the exact hills that inspired Creighton's design of the state seal, but the views on this ride don't quite seem quite right. Art Weber, author of *Ohio State Parks: A Guide to Ohio's State Parks,* suggests that the intersection of Ohio highways 104 and 207, to the west of Great Seal State Park, seems to fit the bill.

Hocking Hills Bike Hike

Number of miles:	13
Approximate pedaling time:	2 hours
Terrain:	Hilly
Traffic:	Can be heavy on summer weekends
Things to see:	Hocking Hills State Park's natural wonders including Ash Cave, Old Man's Cave, Cedar Falls
Facilities:	Picnic areas, water, and toilets at all state park sites; grocery/carry-out stores in South Bloomingville and near Old Man's Cave State Park; camping at Old Man's Cave State Park and nearby private campgrounds; lodging in many private cabins and motels throughout the area.

While cycling in hiking boots is not always recommended, if you don't bring walking shoes on this ride, you will miss the point entirely. Hocking County has the most spectacular scenery in Ohio. Some can be seen from the road, but the best of it is viewed from just off the roadways of this tour.

Hocking Hills State Park is probably the best-known state park in Ohio, and it's easy to see why. There are six park sites in the region, and each is uniquely beautiful. There are waterfalls, gorges, and huge caves, all set in tree-shrouded Appalachian foothills. Creeks tumble through the area, plunging over the cliffs and cutting through the steep gorges. You'll visit three of the park sites on this ride.

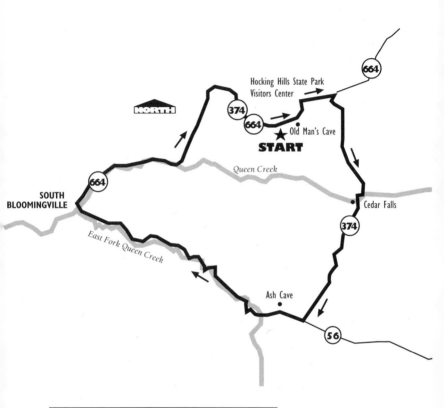

664

Hocking Hills State Park
Visitors Center

374
664

★ Old Man's Cave
START

Queen Creek

664

**SOUTH
BLOOMINGVILLE**

East Fork Queen Creek

Cedar Falls

374

Ash Cave

56

NORTH

Getting There

From Interstate 270, take U.S. Highway 33
south to OH–664. Go south on OH–664
about 12 miles to the Hocking Hills State
Park Visitors Center.

DIRECTIONS at a glance

0.0	Turn right from the visitors center parking lot on OH–374/OH–664.
0.2	Entrance to Old Man's Cave State Park campground is on right.
0.3	Picnic Cafe snack stand is on the right.
0.7	Turn right to continue on OH–374 and begin steep uphill climb.
1.8	Steep downhill.
2.5	Cedar Falls State Park entrance is on right at bottom of hill. Return to the road and turn right to leave Cedar Falls. Begin going uphill immediately.
3.3	Turn left at Y intersection to continue on OH–374. Road goes down steep hill.
4.4	At stop sign at bottom of hill at T intersection, turn right onto OH–56.
4.7	Ash Cave State Park entrances on both sides of road.
7.2	Down steep hill.
8.5	At stop sign at T intersection in South Bloomingville, turn right onto OH–664.
10.1	Climb up steep hill.
11.3	Turn right at Y intersection to continue on OH–664/374.
12.6	Entrance to Old Man's Cave State Park is on right.
13.0	Turn right into visitors center parking lot to end ride.

There is little flat ground to be had on this ride. The roads are well-surfaced but curvy and mostly shoulderless, and weekends often mean heavy traffic. The hiking trails should not be attempted in cycling cleats.

Old Man's Cave is the most popular area in the Hocking Hills park system. The main attraction is a cave that hermit Richard

Rowe reportedly lived in after the Civil War. The cave is easily visible from a bridge over a gorge 100 yards from the visitors center, where the ride starts. Walk a short distance from the visitors center and you can climb into the cave yourself. There are also two waterfalls and several interesting rock formations in the gorge.

You can hike the bottom of the gorge, around much of its rim, or both. If you're feeling adventurous, you can even follow a trail 3 miles to Cedar Falls.

Save the long hike for later, though, because Cedar Falls State Park is only 2.5 miles away by bike. The falls are clearly audible from the parking area, and the hike down to them is a little more than 1.5 miles. There are steps and switchbacks to ease the hike down to the water. Just don't look for cedar trees on your way; early residents mistook the many hemlock trees in the gorge for cedars and misnamed the falls.

A little more than 2 hilly miles away by bike plus a very easy .25 mile on foot is Ash Cave. There are entrances and picnic facilities on both sides of the road, but the trail to the cave is on the right side. Ash Cave is the largest recess cave in Ohio. It is a 700-foot-wide cavity with a Blackhand sandstone overhang 90 feet overhead. The cave stretches 100 feet from its exterior to its deepest point, and a small waterfall drops over the overhang to the valley floor below. Early settlers found huge piles of ashes on the floor of this cave. They were thought to be the remnants of campfires lit by early Indians.

After leaving Ash Cave, there are 8.3 miles remaining on your ride. The town of South Bloomingville, at Mile 8.5, offers a brief respite from the hills and some places to get a bite. Be prepared for a steep, mile-long climb at Mile 10.1. The final steep portion of this ride runs downhill starting at Mile 12.3. Your ride ends at the turnoff to the visitors center at Mile 13.0.

A Little Bit of TOSRV

Number of miles:	13.8
Approximate pedaling time:	1.5 hours
Terrain:	Flat to rolling
Traffic:	Generally light; may be heavy on OH–220 heading into Waverly
Things to see:	Scioto River Valley, part of the original TOSRV route
Facilities:	Restaurants and shopping in Waverly; primitive camping at Lake White State Park, 2 miles south of Waverly

TOSRV, the Tour of the Scioto River Valley, is a two-day 210-mile-long bike tour that happens every Mother's Day weekend. Curiously enough, it started in 1962 as a father-and-son outing. More than thirty-five years later, thousands of riders participate in this Columbus-to-Portsmouth odyssey sponsored by Columbus Outdoor Pursuits. As many as 7,000 riders have taken part each year.

The remarkable success of this event has spurred the development of numerous imitators. There's TOSRV West, TOSRV East, and TOSRVs North and South. When all the simple directions were used up, people created TOSRV Northwest. They then started using state names, such as TOSRV Texas and TOSRV California. Still, there's nothing like the original of any event, and thousands of Ohio cyclists wouldn't miss their annual Mother's Day adventure.

This ride travels on a small stretch of one of the most scenic portions of the TOSRV route, starting in Waverly. It is the part of

NORTH

★ START

WAVERLY

OMEGA

Scioto River

River Rd.

23

104

335

335

51

220

23

Getting There

From Interstate 270, go south on U.S. Highway 23 to Waverly. Turn left onto Clough Street. Waverly High School is on the left in about one block.

DIREC-TIONS at a glance

0.0	Leave Waverly High School by heading out north end of parking lot. Turn right at stop sign onto Second Street/OH–335.
3.9	Veer right to stay on OH–335.
6.5	Turn right onto River Road/County Road 51.
8.1	Turn right at Y intersection to continue on River Road.
11.2	Turn right at stop sign at T intersection on OH–220.
12.2	Waverly limits.
12.5	Cross three sets of railroad tracks.
13.2	Turn left onto Third Street.
13.2	Turn right onto Vine Street.
13.3	Turn right at stop sign at T intersection onto Second Street.
13.4	Cross Market Street to stay on Second Street.
13.8	Cross Clough Street into high school parking lot to end ride.

TOSRV that breaks away from OH–104 and takes to the rolling hills between Chillicothe and Waverly. Don't despair, because the hills are neither terribly steep nor terribly long. On most of them you'll be able to build up enough momentum on the down side to take you over the top of the next hill without straining too hard.

These hills bring you to a ridge from which you will be able to see a ribbon of river and rolling green farmland stretching to the Appalachian foothills to the east. In all too short a distance, you'll turn to the east, cross the Scioto River and then ride a nearly flat road that closely parallels the river almost all the way back to Waverly.

The ride starts in the parking lot at Waverly High School, on

Second Street at Clough Street. Go out the north end of the parking lot, away from Clough Street, and continue north on Second Street/OH–335.

You'll begin rising out of town almost immediately, and the vista of the Scioto Valley opens up to your right in .75 mile as you crest the first hill.

At mile 3.9, veer right to continue on OH–335 (TOSRV veterans will have to avoid the temptation to turn left up the hill). About 2 miles later, you'll cross the Scioto and soon turn south on River Road. River Road has a lot of trees to offer shade, and it often rolls very close to the sparkling river.

The busiest part of this ride is the 2-mile stretch of OH–220 that brings you back to Waverly. About .4 mile from the end of the ride, at the intersection of Second and Market streets, you might like to take one or even two short detours: Baskin-Robbins ice cream shop is one block to the left on Market, and the Pike Museum, open 1:00 to 4:00 P.M. on weekends, is half a block to the right on Market.

As you roll back to the school parking lot at the ride's end, allow your mind to wander back to those roller-coaster hills at the ride's start. Imagine yourself and 4,000 of your closest friends pulling out of Waverly and heading back to Columbus. You rode 105 miles yesterday—and you're sore—but you're having a great time talking with a guy who came all the way from Australia to ride in exotic Ohio.

Now snap yourself out of your reverie and tell yourself, "Maybe next year...."

Ohio's Dirty Secret

Number of miles:	18.4
Approximate pedaling time:	2.5 hours
Terrain:	Rolling to hilly
Surfaces:	Includes 2 miles of gravel road
Traffic:	Very light except in and around Wellston
Things to see:	Buckeye Furnace Historical Site
Facilities:	Restaurants and stores in Wellston; picnic tables at Buckeye Furnace Historical Site; restrooms and water in Buckeye Furnace Museum

Southern Ohio has a dirty secret. Today when you travel there, you see lush valleys choked with huge stands of hardwoods. If you could have seen the area in the late 1800s, you would not have recognized it. Imagine every tree gone for miles in every direction; they were cut to stoke the Buckeye Furnace and feed the unquenchable hunger of industrial progress.

In the nineteenth century the Industrial Revolution roared through the country. The demand for iron ballooned, and southern Ohio came to the rescue. It had ready deposits of iron ore, limestone, and wood. Wood became charcoal, used to heat the mixture of ore and stone. The result was high-grade iron. Soon iron-smelting enterprises such as Buckeye Furnace blanketed the area.

In the late 1800s trains (whose rails were built of southern Ohio iron), drove a spike into the heart of the local furnaces. Low transportation costs allowed large efficient mills in Pittsburgh to ship in ore from Minnesota, coal from West Virginia,

and limestone from Ohio. The local furnaces withered away. The valleys grew back their coats of trees. Huge furnace chimneys deep in the woods now stand in mute testimony to the towns that flourished, made iron, then disappeared into the rugged countryside.

The Ohio Historical Society restored Buckeye Furnace as a monument to this unique chapter in the state's history. It is a fascinating look into a story unfamiliar to most Ohioans. As a bonus, it is in one of the most beautiful parts of the state.

This is the perfect area for a peaceful ride in the countryside. Woods blanket the hillsides, and there are few farms and houses. The streams meandering through the area have reddish water, hinting at the rocks' iron content.

Jackson County is little explored, and many of the roads are unpaved. This ride, however, has only 2 miles of gravel. You will encounter little traffic—whether the roads are paved or not—except in and around Wellston.

Begin at the back of the McDonald's restaurant parking lot in Wellston. Exit the lot by turning right out the back of the lot onto an unmarked alley. (Have a bite to eat at McDonald's in exchange for using the parking lot.) You might also stock up on picnic supplies in Wellston, because it is the only town on the ride.

Buckeye Furnace Historical Site is about 8 miles into the ride. The company store has a short video that tells about the furnace's operation and history. Merchandise found in a typical company store is on display, too. Take some time to walk around the grounds and explore the restored structures. Picnic tables scattered under the tall trees by the parking area provide a pleasant lunch stop.

About .5 mile after crossing the Buckeye Furnace Covered Bridge, the asphalt peters out on Buckeye Road T–165. When the asphalt resumes again at Mile 10.9, the road is known as Goose Run Road.

Pattonsville Road and OH–327 are the hilliest portion of the ride. Be very careful when turning onto 327 from Pattonsville, because the sight lines are very bad.

NORTH

START
McDonald's

Raccoon Creek

S. Maine Ave.

327

32

38

Hiram W. Rd.

124

124

Flint Run

58

Buckeye Furnace
Bridge

Buckeye Furnace
State Memorial

Pattonsville Rd.

Buckeye Rd.

165

Goose Run Rd.

Getting There

From Interstate–70, drive south on
OH–37 to Lancaster, then southeast on
U.S. Highway 33 to Logan. From
Logan, Wellston is about 32 miles
south on OH–93. Turn left into the Mc-
Donald's parking lot on the left of
OH–93/OH–327 in Wellston.

0.0 Turn right out of parking lot onto un-marked alley.

0.0 Turn left at stop sign onto Thirteenth Street (unmarked).

0.0 Turn right at stop sign onto New York Avenue.

0.1 Turn left at stop sign onto Fourteenth Street.

0.6 Turn right at stop sign onto South Maine Avenue.

1.9 Cross OH–32 at stop sign, and continue on Hiram West/County Road 38.

2.9 Turn left at stop sign at T intersection on OH–124.

5.0 Turn right onto Buckeye Furnace Road/CR 58. A sign points the way to Buckeye Furnace.

7.3 Turn right into marked Buckeye Furnace entrance.

7.8 Furnace is on left.

8.0 Parking lot is on right.

8.1 To leave furnace, continue out the road through the historic site, cross 1871 Buckeye Furnace Covered Bridge to stay on rough Buckeye Road T–165.

11.3 Turn right at stop sign at T intersection onto Pattonsville Road, which is hilly but paved.

13.9 Turn right at stop sign at T intersection onto OH–327, which is also somewhat hilly as well. (Watch out for bad sight lines at turn.)

18.4 Turn right into McDonald's parking lot to end ride.

After you cross OH–32 at Mile 16.7, there will be a noticeable increase in traffic. You can expect this heavier traffic for the final 2 miles back into Wellston.

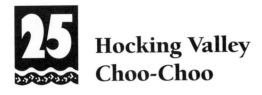

Hocking Valley
Choo-Choo

Number of miles:	29.3
Approximate pedaling time:	3 hours
Terrain:	Almost equally split between flat and hilly
Surface:	Paved roads and rail–trail
Things to see:	Hocking Valley Scenic Railway, Robbins' Crossing, Hocking River Valley
Facilities:	Restaurants and stores in Athens and Nelsonville; camping at Strouds Run State Park, about 5 miles from Athens.

Here's a chance to "ride the rails" of the past and the present on the same day.

This ride through the hill country of southeastern Ohio needn't put off novice cyclists, because it includes a new-in-1997 rail–trail that is virtually flat. The trail parallels the Hocking River for much of the way between Athens and Nelsonville, and passes through shady woods most of the time. If you want to guarantee yourself a flat easy ride, take the trail both ways.

To continue the railroad theme, schedule your ride for a weekend between Memorial Day and October so you can take a relaxing trip on the Hocking Valley Scenic Railway. These historic trains chug along the former Chesapeake & Ohio Railroad through the Hocking River Valley. Bikes are not allowed on the train, so bring a lock to secure your bike at the station.

The train makes a twenty-minute stop at Robbins' Crossing, on the campus of Hocking Technical College. The bike ride will

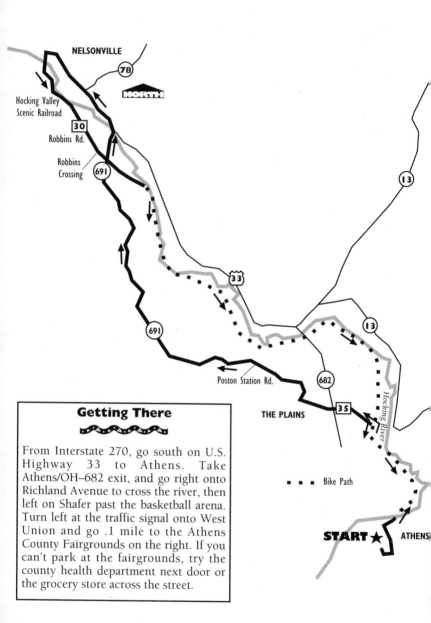

NELSONVILLE

78

NORTH

Hocking Valley
Scenic Railroad

30

Robbins Rd.

Robbins
Crossing

691

691

Poston Station Rd.

13

13

33

682

35

THE PLAINS

Hocking River

Getting There

From Interstate 270, go south on U.S.
Highway 33 to Athens. Take
Athens/OH–682 exit, and go right onto
Richland Avenue to cross the river, then
left on Shafer past the basketball arena.
Turn left at the traffic signal onto West
Union and go .1 mile to the Athens
County Fairgrounds on the right. If you
can't park at the fairgrounds, try the
county health department next door or
the grocery store across the street.

▪ ▪ ▪ Bike Path

START ★ ATHENS

DIRECTIONS at a glance

0.0 Turn left out of fairgrounds onto West Union Street.

0.1 Turn left onto North Shafer Street.

0.4 Turn left at traffic signal onto West State Street.

0.4 Turn right onto Central Avenue.

0.7 Turn left onto Second Street.

0.7 Turn right onto Currier Street and go down short, but steep, hill.

0.8 Multi-use rail–trail begins.

1.5 Cross railroad tracks.

3.3 Turn left off trail past a dark wooden building with ivy growing on it.

3.3 Continue straight at stop sign (start climbing up to next stop sign)

3.4 Turn left at stop sign at Y intersection on Johnson Road/Athens County 7. The road becomes Connett Road after crossing Plains Road.

4.8 Turn right at stop sign at T intersection onto Lemaster Road/CR 246.

5.2 Turn left at stop sign onto Poston Station Road/CR 110.

7.9 Turn right at T intersection onto OH–691.

11.7 Turn right at T intersection to remain on OH–691.

12.6 Turn left at traffic signal at T intersection onto U.S. Highway 33 (*caution*: busy).

13.1 Turn right at Y intersection onto Walnut Street, which is brick.

13.3 Turn right onto Seine Street.

13.3 Turn left onto Poplar Street.

14.2 Continue straight onto Jefferson Street.

14.3 Turn left onto Columbus Street.

14.5 Turn left onto Fulton Road.

14.6 Hocking Valley Scenic Railway is on the left. To leave the depot, turn left out of parking lot onto Fulton Street and cross river.

15.8 Turn left at T intersection onto Robbins Road/CR 30 and immediately cross railroad tracks.

16.2 Robbins' Crossing is on right.

16.3 Turn right just after Robbins' Crossing buildings at The Day Care Connection.

16.4 Turn left onto the rail–trail.

28.5 At end of path veer left onto Currier Street up short steep hill.

28.6 Turn left onto Second Street.

28.6 Turn right onto Central Avenue.

28.9 Turn left onto West State Street.

28.9 Turn right onto North Shafer Street.

29.2 Turn right onto West Union Street.

29.3 Turn right into fairgrounds parking lot to end ride.

---

take you by there, though, and you might wish to make a longer stop on your own. Robbins' Crossing is a special visitors center that serves as a lab for Hocking College students studying interpretive services. On weekend afternoons from Memorial Day through Christmas, students dress in period costume and demonstrate how people lived more than a century ago. You might see men hewing wood, sawing lumber, and splitting rails or women preparing meals or quilting. You might even get a chance to try your hand at making wood shingles or dipping candles.

You'll reach the rail–trail less than a mile after you start your ride. When you turn left off the trail at Mile 3.3 in The Plains, the road is rough, with lots of gravel, and goes up a hill. A little more than 9 hilly miles later, you'll roll into Nelsonville. Edwards Grocery, at Mile 13.5, offers a chance to stop and buy a picnic lunch if you're planning on taking a train trip. Be sure to turn around and look back when you turn onto Fulton Road to see the impressive mural of a train.

You'll ride up a hill out of town and reach Robbins' Crossing at Mile 16.2. The rail–trail is a mere .2 mile later, and you'll have a 12-mile respite from the hills. Then after a short steep push out of the river valley, you'll be on Athens' city streets less than a mile from the end of your ride.

If you have time, take a walk downtown. Athens is a true college town—downtown goes right up to the doors of Ohio University—and it's also in a beautiful setting. In addition, there are plenty of restaurants from which to choose.

Lock, Stock, and Barrel

Number of miles:	21.1
Approximate pedaling time:	2.5 hours
Terrain:	Rolling to moderately hilly
Traffic:	Very light, except on state highways
Things to see:	Muskingum River, manual lock system
Facilities:	Picnic tables, grills, latrines, and drinking water at locks 6 and 7; stores and restaurants in Stockport and McConnelsville

The Muskingum River is the largest river lying solely within Ohio. At 112 miles long, it stretches from Coshocton south to Marietta, where it drains into the Ohio River. If a drop of water lands on Ohio, it has a one in five chance of finding its way into the Muskingum.

In the golden age of canals, the river was channelized so it could play a part in the ferrying of men and materials. Today the Muskingum is designated a state park, and it is a favorite haunt of recreational boaters and anglers. It also provides a fascinating bike ride.

This ride is a trek along the Muskingum through the scenic Ohio hill country. In spring and summer you'll traverse a green landscape sliced by a sparkling ribbon of blue; in fall, that blue ribbon will reflect the splashes of color painted on the trees by Mother Nature.

If you're riding on a weekend between April and November, be sure to check out one or both of the locks on this ride. The

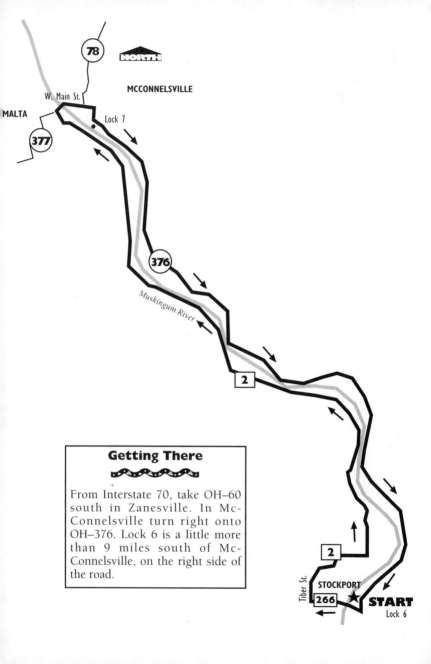

78

NORTH

MCCONNELSVILLE

W. Main St.

MALTA

377

• Lock 7

376

Muskingum River

2

Getting There

From Interstate 70, take OH–60 south in Zanesville. In Mc-Connelsville turn right onto OH–376. Lock 6 is a little more than 9 miles south of Mc-Connelsville, on the right side of the road.

2

Tiber St.

STOCKPORT

266

★ START

Lock 6

0.0	Go out driveway from Lock 6 parking lot.
0.2	Turn right at stop sign at T intersection onto OH–376.
0.2	Turn right at stop sign onto OH–266 and cross river.
0.9	Turn right onto Tiber Street.
1.4	Morgan County Road 2 marker on sweeping right curve.
2.2	Turn left at Y intersection to remain on CR 2.
3.0	Turn right at Y intersection to remain on CR 2. Be careful on rough downhill.
9.9	McConnelsville lock and dam are visible on the right.
10.7	Turn right at stop sign onto narrow bridge and cross river.
10.8	Turn right at traffic signal onto West Main Street.
11.3	Turn right at traffic signal onto North Street/OH–376.
11.6	Turn left at T intersection to stay on OH–376.
11.7	Turn right to enter park at Lock 7. To leave, turn right onto OH–376.
20.9	Turn right onto Lock 6 access road.
21.1	End ride in Lock 6 parking lot.

small parks at the locks offer great views of the river and are good places for picnicking. In addition you'll want to check out the locking operation. The system of ten dams and eleven locks connecting the Muskingum to the Ohio & Erie Canal at Dresden was designed by West Point graduate Samuel Curtis and opened in 1841. To this day, the sandstone locks and their big wooden gates are operated manually. The lockmasters are happy to explain the process as they perform their duties.

This ride is between locks 6 and 7 and starts in Stockport.

Although the route never leaves the river valley, it is moderately hilly. On the east side of the river you'll be on a state highway, which means your way will be smoother and boast more gentle terrain than that on the west bank. The trade-off, however, will be more car traffic and less shade. The roads on the river's west side are at times rough and offer sharper ups and downs but have practically no traffic. You will also pass through a tunnel of trees for much of the ride.

After leaving Lock 6, you'll immediately cross the river into Stockport. As you head out of town, you'll turn right at the bottom of a hill onto Tiber Street at Mile 0.9. Half a mile later, you'll see that Tiber has become Morgan County Road 2 as you round a sweeping right curve.

At Mile 3.0, after you turn right at the Y intersection, there is a rough hill down to the river bank. You'll spend the remaining ride on this side of the Muskingum very close to the river. Notice that there are lots of small vacation cabins at river's edge. Sitting in the yards and on the water's surface will be small portable piers made of decking attached to what look like barrels.

The bridge across the river at Malta is very narrow. Assert yourself and take up a lane so no drivers can force you dangerously close to the side of the bridge.

After you pass the Civil War monument in McConnelsville, the remainder of the ride will be on OH–376. Lock 7, at Mile 11.7, offers a respite from the saddle about halfway through the ride.

Lose Your Head in Marietta

Distance:	6.2
Approximate pedaling time:	1 hour
Terrain:	Mostly flat with some small rises
Traffic:	Busy in some parts of this urban ride
Surface:	Rough with many brick streets
Things to see:	Marietta; Ohio and Muskingum rivers; Campus Martius; Ohio River, doll and toy, miniature train, Fearing House, and other museums; historic buildings and riverboats; Marietta College; river cruises; trolley tour; Indian mounds
Facilities:	Restaurants and stores are plentiful in this urban area; bike shop on Third Street between Scammel and Wooster Streets

Marietta was named after Marie Antoinette, and like her, you too will lose your head looking at all the city's historic sites. The city is Ohio's and the Northwest Territory's first settlement; it was founded in 1788 by Connecticut veterans of the Revolutionary War. In fact it was the first such settlement west of the original thirteen colonies.

Its location at the confluence of the Ohio and Muskingum rivers brought Marietta quick prominence as a transportation center, and today the city revels in its riverboat heritage, with sternwheeler cruises offered on the *Valley Gem,* old-time theater productions on the *Becky Thatcher Showboat,* and an annual

Sternwheeler Festival in September. Even the old houses with their big front porches resemble sternwheelers.

Marietta is surrounded by steep wooded hillsides that put on glorious colors in the fall. This ride, however, keeps you in the city, near the rivers. There is, consequently, no real climbing or descending. Be prepared, however, for a bumpy ride, because many of the streets retain their brick paving along with their charm.

Also be prepared to spend a full afternoon on this ride, because there are many plaques describing the historic sites. Stops at the various museums also will add time to your tour.

At the beginning of your ride, stop at the fountain in Ohio River Front Park for a panoramic view of the Ohio River. There are many plaques to read by the fountain and in the parking lot behind it. From the fountain head out on Front Street. When you pass between pillars with eagles on them several blocks later, you will pass Muskingum River Park on the left. Look for a Civil War statue and a sandstone sculpture by Gutzon Borglum (of Mount Rushmore fame) called *The Start West* as you ride by the park.

The Ohio River Museum, at Mile 0.9, focuses on river life. It includes boats such as a flatboat barge and one of the last steam towboats of the Mark Twain era.

One-tenth of a mile later, you will turn onto Sacra Via, originally a walled path built by the Hopewell Indians (circa A.D. 900) to a holy mound later named Quadranaou by the American settlers. You will pass the remnant of the mound at Mile 1.5.

You'll pass two more mounds: At Mile 1.8, the Washington County Public Library sits on the remnant of a Hopewell Indian mound; and .3 mile later you will start circling Mound Cemetery, which has a 30-foot-high mound in its center. You might want to explore the cemetery when you reach the entrance on Fifth Street. If you wish you can climb the steps to the mound's top. Take a look at the headstones in the cemetery. There is a greater number of Revolutionary War officers buried here than at any other cemetery in the nation.

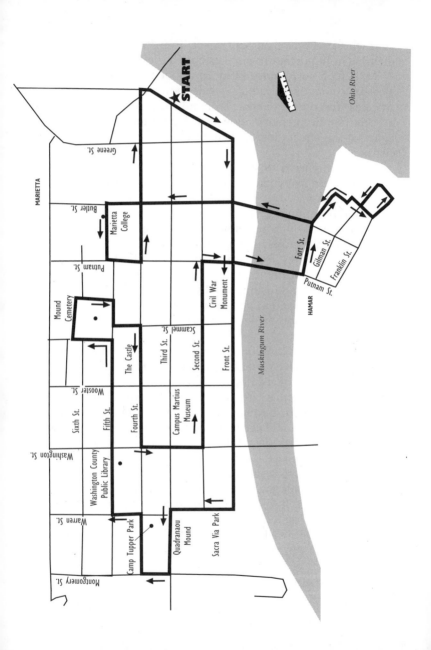

START

NORTH

Ohio River

Muskingum River

MARIETTA

HAMAR

Greene St.

Butler St.

Marietta College

Putnam St.

Mound Cemetery

The Castle

Third St.

Scammel St.

Second St.

Civil War Monument

Front St.

Wooster St.

Fourth St.

Campus Martius Museum

Fifth St.

Sixth St.

Washington St.

Washington County Public Library

Warren St.

Camp Tupper Park

Quadranaou Mound

Sacra Via Park

Montgomery St.

Fort St.

Gilman St.

Franklin St.

Putnam St.

0.0 To start ride turn left from parking lot onto Ohio Street.

0.2 Hop curb and walk or ride to fountain. From the fountain, go out onto Front Street, which dead ends on Ohio Street. (Be careful: oncoming traffic does not stop.)

0.9 *Valley Gem* sternwheeler cruise boat is on left.

0.9 Ohio River Museum is on left. To leave museum, turn left onto Front Street.

1.0 Turn right onto Sacra Via.

1.2 Turn left at stop sign at T intersection onto Third Street.

1.3 Turn right onto Montgomery Street.

1.4 Turn right onto Fourth Street at stop sign.

1.5 Remnant of Quadranaou mound is on right.

1.6 Turn left onto Warren Street.

1.7 Turn right at stop sign onto Fifth Street.

2.1 Turn left on Tupper Street and start circling Mound Cemetery.

2.2 Turn right onto Sixth Street.

2.4 Turn right onto Cutler Street.

2.5 Turn right at stop sign onto Fifth Street, then turn right to enter the cemetery. To leave cemetery, go straight out entry gate onto Scammel Street.

2.6 Turn right at stop sign onto Fourth Street.

2.7 The Castle (built in 1855) on right is open for public tours.

Getting There

From Interstate 77, go south on OH–7. Turn left on Fourth Street, then right on Hart Street, which quickly becomes Ohio Street. Park on left in Ohio River Front Park under the Ohio River bridge.

2.9 Turn left at traffic signal onto Washington Street.

3.1 Turn right at traffic signal onto Second Street, then left into Campus Martius Museum. To leave museum, turn right out of driveway onto Second Street.

3.7 Turn right at traffic signal onto Putnam Street. Washington County Courthouse is on left just before turn.

3.8 Continue straight at traffic signal to cross Muskingum River.

3.9 Turn left immediately after getting off bridge onto Fort Street (caution: busy area). Fort Street is right on the river.

4.1 Turn right onto Fort Square, site of a 1785 U.S. military fort. Continue on Fort Square, which takes a ninety-degree right turn.

4.1 Turn left onto Crawford Street.

4.2 Turn right onto Market Street.

4.3 Turn left at traffic signal onto Franklin Street.

4.5 Turn left at stop sign at T intersection onto Virginia Street.

4.6 Monument from France is on right. Road name changes to Gilman Street after veering sharply left.

4.8 Turn right at stop sign onto Maple Street.

4.9 As you approach end of Maple Street, go right onto brick path in front of Harmar Station miniature train museum and the trains. Follow path onto trestle foot bridge to Marietta. (Path is narrow; sign suggests walking bikes.)

5.0 Go straight off bridge through parking lot.

5.1 Turn left out of parking lot onto Butler Street.

5.5 Turn left onto pedestrian mall through the Marietta College campus.

5.6 Turn left onto Putnam Street.

5.6 Turn left at traffic signal onto Fourth Street.

6.1 Turn right onto Hart Street, which soon becomes Ohio Street.

6.2 Turn left into parking lot at Ohio River Front Park to end ride.

Campus Martius (Latin for "Field of Mars") was the civilian fort built to protect the Americans who came to settle the region. The Campus Martius Museum is on the site of the fort at Mile 3.1 and focuses on settlement and migration in Ohio from 1780 to 1970.

Next you'll cross the Muskingum River to Harmar Village, which at one time seceded from Marietta. Now this village, the site of the first fort in Marietta, is a sleepy hamlet. Sleepy or not, the historic houses, museums, and riverfront views are worth the trip.

Of special interest is a mural on a pump house overlooking the confluence of the two rivers at Mile 4.1. It was developed by students at neighboring Harmar Elementary School and painted by Geoff Schenkel. This spot also offers a wonderful view of the Ohio River. Half a mile later, you'll pass a stone monument on the right. This gift from France commemorates that nation's claiming of these lands in 1749 following an expedition of exploration.

Once you cross the Muskingum River back to Marietta, you will ride through part of the Marietta College campus before returning to your starting point.

Mad Anthony Wayne Ride

Number of miles:	19.3
Approximate pedaling time:	2 hours
Terrain:	Flat to gently rolling farmland
Traffic:	Generally light, except on federal and state routes
Things to see:	Magnificent churches, Fort Recovery monument, Fort Recovery State Memorial
Facilities:	Restaurants and stores in villages of St. Henry and Fort Recovery; picnic shelter, water, and restrooms at Fort Recovery State Memorial

The gently rolling farmland of Mercer County once was the site of deadly clashes between Indians and settlers. Now you can easily ride along the peaceful lightly traveled roads and trace the path General "Mad" Anthony Wayne took when he exacted a terrible revenge on the Indians who were harassing American settlers and troops.

In the late 1700s Indians, frustrated by the increasing numbers of American settlers and goaded by British officials, frequently attacked settlers and the troops sent to quell the troubles on the frontier.

The most devastating of these attacks occurred just before sunrise on November 4, 1791, on the banks of the Wabash River in what is now Fort Recovery. Chiefs Little Turtle and Blue Jacket and renegade Simon Girty led 1,000 to 1,500 Indians from seven tribes against American troops under the command

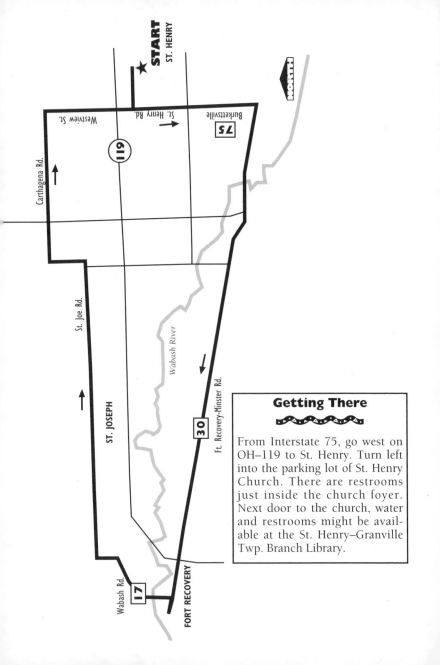

START
ST. HENRY

NORTH

Westview St.

St. Henry Rd.

Burkettsville

75

611

Carthagena Rd.

St. Joe Rd.

Wabash River

Ft. Recovery-Minster Rd.

30

ST. JOSEPH

Wabash Rd.

17

FORT RECOVERY

Getting There

From Interstate 75, go west on OH–119 to St. Henry. Turn left into the parking lot of St. Henry Church. There are restrooms just inside the church foyer. Next door to the church, water and restrooms might be available at the St. Henry–Granville Twp. Branch Library.

DIREC-TIONS at a glance

0.0	Turn left onto Main Street/OH–119 to leave St. Henry Catholic Church.
0.3	Turn left at Y intersection to stay on Main Street (OH–119 goes right).
0.5	Turn left at stop sign at T intersection on Westview Street.

1.3 Road becomes Burkettsville–St. Henry Road/Mercer County Road 75.

2.2 Turn right at stop sign at T intersection on Fort Recovery–Minster Road/CR 30.

8.5 Fort Recovery limits.

8.9 Continue straight; road becomes Boundary Street.

9.1 Fort Recovery monument is on left.

9.3 Continue straight across Wayne Street.

9.3 Dead end at Fort Recovery State Memorial. Museum is to left. To leave fort, go back out Boundary Street.

9.5 Turn left at stop sign onto First Street.

9.9 Cross railroad tracks.

10.0 Turn right at stop sign onto Wabash Road/CR 17.

10.9 Turn right onto St. Joe Road/Township Road 54.

12.3 Pass St. Joseph Catholic Church.

12.5 Cross railroad tracks.

14.9 Turn left at stop sign at Y intersection to remain on St. Joe/TR 54.

15.4 Turn right onto Carthagena Road/TR 60.

17.5 Turn right at stop sign onto Burkettsville–St. Henry Road/CR 75.

18.7 Turn left onto Main Street.

19.0 Road merges with Highway 119.

19.3 Turn right into St. Henry Catholic Church parking lot to end ride.

of Northwest Territory Governor and General Arthur St. Clair. The surprised troops were overwhelmed, and 630 soliders died in battle while 250 women accompanying the expedition were either killed or taken prisoner.

A post-defeat investigation found that St. Clair's troops were ill-trained, ill-equipped, and totally unprepared for a surprise attack. President George Washington decided to send Wayne to the Northwest Territory to redeem the nation's reputation and secure the area for settlers. The general the Indians called "the man who never sleeps" trained his 2,600-man army intensively before traveling north from Fort Washington (now Cincinnati) to the Wabash River in 1793. En route Wayne's troops built Fort GreenVille. From there, troops were detached to the Wabash River battleground to bury the bones of the dead and build Fort Recovery.

On June 30, 1794, the new fort was attacked by one of the largest forces of Indians that ever engaged the American army in battle. The well-trained American troops prevailed on the site of previous disaster. Two months later, the war ended when Wayne's troops won the Battle of Fallen Timbers. This victory led to the signing of the Treaty of GreenVille in 1795. The Indians agreed to give up their claim to all lands south of what we know as Fort Recovery–Minster Road in exchange for $20,000 in merchandise and an annual payment of $9,500. This treaty, more than any other event, is what opened up the territory to Americans and led to Ohio's statehood only eight years later.

Your ride begins in the parking lot of St. Henry Catholic Church. If the church is open, check out its stained-glass windows. Fort Recovery, almost halfway through this ride, offers the standard fast-food places to eat and drink as well as historic sites to visit. At Mile 9.1, take some time to explore the square with the obelisk, ordered by Congress to honor those who died in the battles of 1791 and 1794. Just .2 mile later you'll find a museum and partly reconstructed fort at the Fort Recovery State Memorial. The park here is a good site for a picnic.

This region is dotted with Catholic churches built in the area by the many German farmers who settled here after the original forest was cleared. The land is flat, so several tall steeples are often visible from one spot. On your way back to St. Henry, you might stop to count the steeples towering above the corn and soybeans.

Biketoberfest

Number of miles:	23
Approximate pedaling time:	2.5 hours
Terrain:	Flat
Traffic:	Very light except on federal and state routes
Things to see:	Bicycle Museum of America; Lake Loramie State Park; villages of New Bremen, Minster, and Fort Loramie
Facilities:	Restaurants and stores in New Bremen, Minster, and Fort Loramie; picnic shelters, restrooms, and water at Lions Club Park, New Bremen; beach, picnic tables, water, restrooms, and camping at Lake Loramie State Park

Say *"Prosit!"* to cycling in west-central Ohio, where at the right time of year you can sample German culture at one of the largest Oktoberfests for miles around.

Germans fleeing religious persecution settled this area of Auglaize and Shelby counties in the 1830s. Protestants banded together to form Bremen, now New Bremen, while Catholics settled just a few miles to the south and formed Minster and Fort Loramie.

Many of these Germans emigrated with little more than faith, a willingness to work hard, and a sense of order. All can be appreciated on this ride, in magnificent churches and well maintained prosperous farms and villages.

You'll begin this ride in New Bremen's Lions Club Park,

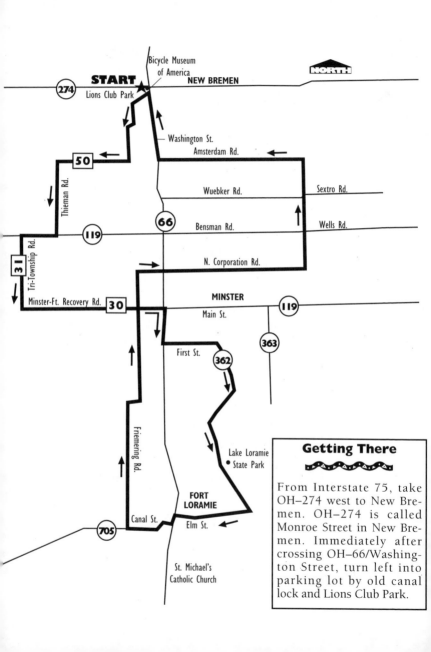

Bicycle Museum of America

START

NORTH

NEW BREMEN

274

Lions Club Park

Washington St.

Amsterdam Rd.

50

Thieman Rd.

Wuebker Rd.

Sextro Rd.

66

Bensman Rd.

Wells Rd.

119

31

Tri-Township Rd.

N. Corporation Rd.

Minster-Ft. Recovery Rd.

30

MINSTER

119

Main St.

363

First St.

362

Friemering Rd.

Lake Loramie
• State Park

FORT
LORAMIE

Canal St.

Elm St.

705

St. Michael's
Catholic Church

Getting There

From Interstate 75, take OH–274 west to New Bremen. OH–274 is called Monroe Street in New Bremen. Immediately after crossing OH–66/Washington Street, turn left into parking lot by old canal lock and Lions Club Park.

0.0   Keeping the canal lock and park on your right, head south out of parking lot on Canal Street.

0.1   Turn right at stop sign at T intersection onto Plum Street.

0.4   Turn left at stop sign at T intersection onto South Herman Street.

0.7   Turn right at stop sign at T intersection onto Erie Road/Auglaize County 47.

1.2   Turn right at stop sign at T intersection onto Amsterdam Road/CR 50.

1.2   Cross rough railroad tracks with caution.

2.2   Turn left onto unmarked Thieman Road.

3.2   Turn right at stop sign at T intersection onto OH–119.

3.7   Turn left onto Tri-Township Road/Township Road 31.

4.7   Turn left at stop sign at T intersection on Minster Fort Recovery Road/CR 30.

6.1   Minster limit. Road name changes to West Fourth Street in town.

6.2   Cross railroad tracks.

6.7   Turn right at traffic light onto Main Street/OH–66.

7.2   Turn left onto First Street/OH–362.

8.2   Start to pass Lake Loramie State Park picnic areas.

10.0   Veer left to remain on OH–362.

10.0   Entrance to Lake Loramie State Park beach is on left (enter and bear right to beach parking). To leave beach, veer left out of parking lot, then left onto OH–362.

10.2   Veer left to stay on OH–362.

10.6   Turn right at stop sign at T intersection to continue on OH–362/Fort Loramie Swanders Road.

11.1   Fort Loramie limit. Road becomes Elm Street in town.

11.5   St. Michael's Catholic Church is on right.

11.7   Cross OH–66 at traffic signal then immediately turn left onto Canal Street. (Canal Park is on left.)

11.8   Turn right at stop sign onto OH–705.

12.3 Turn right onto Friemering Road/Shelby County 94.

14.1 Turn right at stop sign at T intersection onto Dirkson Road/TR 98.

14.3 Road turns sharply left and becomes Friemering again.

15.0 Turn left at stop sign at T intersection onto First Street/Minster Egypt Pike.

15.0 Turn right onto Cleveland Street.

16.0 Turn right at stop sign at T intersection onto West Seventh Street.

16.4 Cross North Main Street/OH–66 at traffic signal. Street becomes North Corporation Road/Township Highway 36 out of town.

18.4 Turn left at stop sign at T intersection onto East Shelby 71.

19.9 Turn left onto Amsterdam Road/CR 50.

21.9 Turn right at stop sign onto OH–66, which becomes Washington Street in New Bremen.

22.7 Turn left at traffic signal onto Plum Street.

22.8 Turn right onto Canal Street.

22.9 Continue straight at stop sign and pass old canal lock.

23.0 Veer left into parking lot to end ride.

---

which is along the old Miami & Erie Canal. Before wheeling away, though, take a trip into the history of the bicycle by walking around the corner to 7 West Monroe Street, the new home of the Bicycle Museum of America.

The museum's collection of bikes from the early 1800s to the present is one of the largest private collections in the world. The museum opened in July 1997 with hobby horses, boneshakers, ordinaries, safeties, tricycles, lightweights, racers, mountain bikes, and even banana-seat children's bicycles on display.

After wondering how early cyclists could keep their traction (and their bones intact) rattling across unpaved roads on steel-rimmed wheels, head back to your bike to take off for a very easy ride on flat paved roads. You will pedal through lush green soybean and corn fields, along one of the lakes dug as a feeder for the canal, and through neat pleasant villages.

On a hot day, you might turn left at Mile 10 to have a picnic in the shade or take a swim at Lake Loramie State Park. Traffic might be a bit heavy here on summer weekends, because the attractive beach and campground are quite popular.

It's worth a few minutes to pull over at Mile 11.5 in Fort Loramie to take a close look at the statues over the main door of St. Michael's Catholic Church. Just before you turn out of town on OH–705, there is a grocery store to the right, should you need to get something to eat.

You'll pass through Minster yet again before you reach New Bremen, so if you're riding on the first weekend of October, you'll have a hard time resisting the lure of Minster's Oktoberfest.

About 2 miles out of Minster is Baker's Bike Shop (if your bike needs any attention). From here, 5 more easy miles will bring you back to Lions Club Park in New Bremen.

Ride Back in Time

Number of miles:	32
Approximate pedaling time:	3 hours
Terrain:	Gently rolling
Traffic:	Light except on state routes
Things to see:	Greenville City Park, including the Altar of Peace monument; pleasant countryside; Union City, Indiana; Union City, Ohio
Facilities:	Restaurants and stores in Greenville and both Union cities; snack bar, water, restrooms, and picnic shelters in Greenville City Park

This ride is a foray back in time, both literally and historically. The starting point, Greenville, played an important role in the settlement of the Northwest Territory, part of which eventually became Ohio.

After his decisive defeat of the Indians in the 1794 Battle of Fallen Timbers on the Maumee River, General "Mad" Anthony Wayne invited 1,100 Indians to Fort GreeneVille—the site of present-day Greenville—to discuss and sign a treaty. On August 3, 1795, after fifty days of feasts and ceremonies, the Indians agreed to give up about three-quarters of what is now Ohio for $20,000 in merchandise and an annual payment of $9,500. The treaty line, north of which was designated as Indian territory and south of which was open to settlement by whites, today is known as Fort Recovery–Minster Road. During this ride you will stay south of the treaty line, never drawing closer than about 14 miles to the "forbidden" territory.

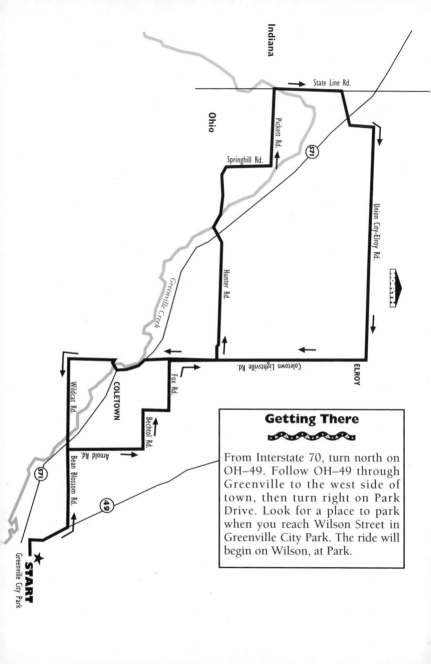

Indiana

Ohio

State Line Rd.

Pickett Rd.

Springhill Rd.

571

Union City-Elroy Rd.

Hunter Rd.

Greenville Creek

ELROY

Coletown Lightsville Rd.

COLETOWN

Fox Rd.

Wildcat Rd.

Bechtol Rd.

Arnold Rd.

Bean Blossom Rd.

571

49

Getting There

From Interstate 70, turn north on OH–49. Follow OH–49 through Greenville to the west side of town, then turn right on Park Drive. Look for a place to park when you reach Wilson Street in Greenville City Park. The ride will begin on Wilson, at Park.

START
Greenville City Park

0.0 Turn west toward OH–49 on Park Drive.

0.7 Turn right at stop sign at T intersection onto OH–49, which has a small paved shoulder.

1.5 Turn left onto Beanblossom Road and immediately cross railroad tracks.

3.0 Turn right at stop sign at T intersection onto Arnold Road.

4.5 Turn left at stop sign at T intersection onto Bechtol Road/Township Road 199.

5.3 Turn right at stop sign at T intersection onto unmarked McMecham Road. Schoolhouse-turned-shed is on left.

5.8 Turn left at stop sign at T intersection onto Fox Road/TR 278.

6.7 Turn right at stop sign at T intersection onto Coletown–Lightsville Road.

7.7 Turn left on Cox Road/TR 50.

10.1 Cross OH–571 at stop sign. Road immediately becomes Converse Road/TR 122.

12.0 Turn right at stop sign at T intersection onto unmarked Springhill Road.

12.9 Turn left at stop sign at T intersection onto Pickett Road.

13.9 Turn right at stop sign at T intersection onto Ohio–Indiana State Line Road.

15.1 Turn left at stop sign on Main Street.

15.2 Turn right at stop sign and red flasher onto Indiana Highway 28/Columbia Street.

15.2 Cross two sets of railroad tracks.

15.3 Turn right at traffic light onto Pearl Street.

15.4 Cross the state line back into Ohio.

16.5 Turn right onto Union City–Elroy Road.

21.0 Turn right at stop sign at T intersection onto Coletown–Lightsville Road.

21.1 Cross two sets of railroad tracks at stop sign.

25.4 Turn left at stop sign at T intersection onto OH–571.

26.2 Turn left onto New Madison–Coletown Road.

27.1 Turn left onto Wildcat Road/TR 89.

28.7 Turn right at stop sign at T intersection onto OH–571.

28.8 Turn left onto Arnold Road.

28.9 Turn right onto Beanblossom Road.

30.4 Cautiously cross railroad tracks, then turn right at stop sign at T intersection onto OH–49.

31.2 Turn left onto West Park Drive.

32.0 Turn left onto Wilson Street to end ride.

Take time before or after your ride to have a picnic at Greenville City Park. This pleasant gathering place has ponds, many picnic shelters, snack bar, horseshoe pitches, and ducks, geese and peacocks. If you walk to the bottom of the park and cross Mud Creek on the pedestrian bridge, then follow the brick path for several hundred feet, you will come upon the Altar of Peace. This isolated memorial was built to commemorate the treaty that opened up the Northwest Territory to white settlement.

This ride is a pleasant spin into gently rolling lightly traveled farmland dotted by groves of hardwood trees. The neat farms are planted mostly in soybeans, making it easy to look out over the land and drink in the views. Don't miss some of the creative touches of man along the way: a one-room schoolhouse built in 1896 currently in use as a shed at Mile 5.3; a "monster" guarding a barn labeled Roll's Roost at Mile 7.9; and an old schoolhouse with its bell tower intact serving as a family home at Mile 28.3.

You also will visit a twin city straddling the Indiana/Ohio border 15 miles into the ride. Eastern Indiana does not adopt daylight-saving time, so if you ride here in the summer, you will experience what is known by the locals as "slow time": Union City, Indiana, is an hour behind Union City, Ohio. This means you can stop for a bite to eat at one of the fast-food places in Union City, Indiana, and a few minutes later, after crossing the Ohio border, stop at the A&W Root Beer stand for dessert—more than an hour later, by the watch!

Castles and Caverns

Number of miles:	9.2
Approximate pedaling time:	1 hour
Terrain:	Rolling with a few steep hills
Traffic:	Generally light, except on state highways
Things to see:	Piatt Castles, Ohio Caverns
Facilities:	Stores, restaurants, ice cream parlor, bed-and-breakfast inn, and bike shop in West Liberty; picnic facilities, restrooms, and water at Lions Community Park and Ohio Caverns

West Liberty is a sleepy little village between Urbana and Bellefontaine on U.S. Highway 68. It is nestled in an area of Ohio that is not too flat and not too hilly, a region the Shawnee Indians called Mac-A-Cheek.

This 9-mile-long ride through rolling hills and fields has some architectural and natural surprises. In addition, there's a sprinkling of craft shops along the way. Your adventure starts in the city park, which all Ohio towns of this size seem to have. Park near first base and ride on out of town.

In about a mile, you will come to your first treat, Castle Mac-A-Cheek. This is a Norman–French-style chateau built in 1868 by Civil War General Abram S. Piatt. The castle has elaborate woodwork and frescoed ceilings plus portraits, books, and Indian artifacts inside. Tours are offered from March through October.

As you continue after Castle Mac-A-Cheek, you'll pass

Pioneer Cabin, which was a stop on the Underground Railroad, and the Piatt Family Cemetery.

You'll do some climbing after you turn onto Highway 507, especially on Highway 245/Mount Tabor Road. Your reward will be good views of the surrounding farmland.

If you're interested in cooling off in the fifty-four-degree Ohio Caverns, turn right at Mile 3.9. You'll meander through the parklike grounds of the caverns, avoiding the steep uphill car entrance, before coming to the building housing the store and cave entrance. To leave the caverns, go downhill out the car entrance, keeping the general store and cave entrance on your right. At the end of the driveway, turn right on Mount Tabor Road.

You'll have a short, steep uphill after turning onto County Road 171, and a rough downhill after turning onto Township Road 166.

At Mile 7.6, a sharp right will bring you to Castle Mac-O-Chee, a Flemish-style castle completed in 1881 by Donn Piatt, the brother of Abram Piatt. Beautiful woodwork and a collection of European and Asian furnishings grace the castle's interior. Again, tours are offered from March through October.

Castle Mac-O-Chee is your signal that your hill-climbing is done and your ride is nearly finished. An easy spin of slightly more than 1.5 miles will bring you back to Lions Community Park.

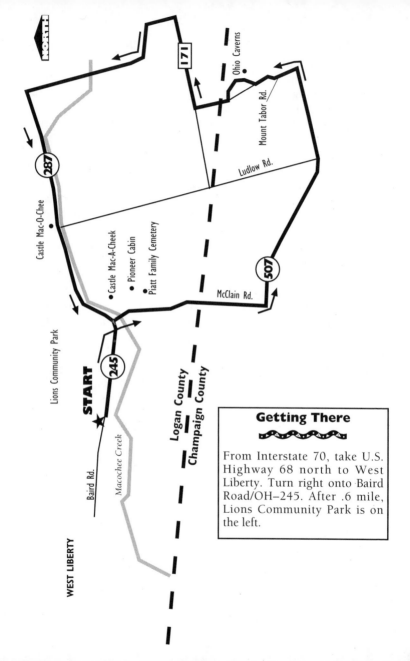

NORTH

171

Ohio Caverns

Mount Tabor Rd.

287

Ludlow Rd.

Castle Mac-O-Chee

Castle Mac-A-Cheek
Pioneer Cabin
Piatt Family Cemetery

507

McClain Rd.

Lions Community Park

245

START

Macochee Creek

Baird Rd.

WEST LIBERTY

Logan County
Champaign County

Getting There

From Interstate 70, take U.S. Highway 68 north to West Liberty. Turn right onto Baird Road/OH–245. After .6 mile, Lions Community Park is on the left.

0.0   Turn left onto Baird Road/OH–245 from Lions Community Park.

0.7   Turn right onto McClain Road/Township Road 112.

0.9   Castle Mac-A-Cheek is on left. To return to route, turn left out of driveway onto McClain Road/TR 112.

0.9   Pioneer Cabin is on left.

1.2   Piatt Family Cemetery is on left.

1.9   Turn left onto OH–507.

3.7   Turn left onto OH–245/Mount Tabor Road.

3.9   To go to Ohio Caverns, turn right into bus entrance. To leave the caverns, continue downhill out auto entrance and turn right onto OH–245/Mount Tabor Road.

4.6   Turn right at stop sign at T intersection onto County Road 171.

5.3   Turn left onto TR 166.

5.5   Veer left to remain on TR 166.

6.6   Turn left at stop sign at T intersection onto OH–287.

7.6   Castle Mac-O-Chee is on the right. To return to the route, turn right out of driveway onto OH–287.

7.6   Continue straight across intersection onto OH–245/Baird Road.

9.2   Turn right into Lions Community Park to end ride.

Bridges of Preble County

Number of miles:	29.4
Approximate pedaling time:	3 hours
Terrain:	Gently rolling with a few hills
Traffic:	Generally light, except on federal and state routes and on the Interstate 70 overpass
Things to see:	Historic covered bridges, rhea farm, rolling farmland and woods
Facilities:	Restaurants and stores in downtown Eaton and north of town by Interstate 70; restrooms, water, and picnic area in Lewisburg Community Park in summer

Preble County has escaped the urban sprawl that has overtaken many Ohio counties. It lies placidly on the Indiana border while life whizzes by at 65 m.p.h. on Interstate 70. Preble County's misfortune—at least according to the local chamber of commerce—is the cyclist's good luck. The quiet roads have been easy on a number of covered bridges that certainly would have been replaced by now in urban Montgomery County just to the east. Those same quiet roads will be easy on you as you visit some of Preble County's eight covered bridges.

Preble County does not now—nor did it ever—have the most covered bridges in Ohio. That honor belongs to Fairfield County, which once had 279 and now has sixteen such spans. Preble County, however, has several bridges of note that are passed or crossed during this ride.

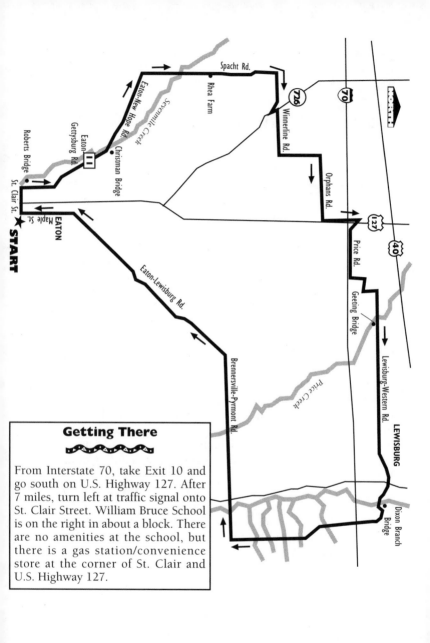

NORTH

Spacht Rd.

Rhea Farm

Eaton-New Hope Rd.

Sevenmile Creek

Eaton-Gettrysburg Rd.

Roberts Bridge

Christman Bridge

St. Clair St.

Maple St.

START

EATON

Eaton-Lewisburg Rd.

Brennersville-Pyrmont Rd.

Winnerline Rd.

Orphans Rd.

Price Rd.

Geeting Bridge

Price Creek

Lewisburg-Western Rd.

LEWISBURG

Dixon Branch Bridge

Getting There

From Interstate 70, take Exit 10 and go south on U.S. Highway 127. After 7 miles, turn left at traffic signal onto St. Clair Street. William Bruce School is on the right in about a block. There are no amenities at the school, but there is a gas station/convenience store at the corner of St. Clair and U.S. Highway 127.

0.0   Turn left from William Bruce School parking lot onto St. Clair Street.

0.2   Turn right onto South Beech Street. Roberts Bridge is on left.

0.5   Turn left at stop sign onto Decatur Street.

0.7   Turn right at stop sign onto Park Street.

1.0   Cross busy railroad track.

1.6   Cross Lexington Road. Road becomes Eaton–Gettysburg Road/Preble County 11.

2.5   Turn left at Y intersection on Eaton–New Hope Road/ Township Road 142.

2.6   Cross Christman Bridge.

4.0   Turn right onto Spacht Road/TR 143.

4.9   Cross Eaton–Gettysburg Road at stop sign. Take care: road is at a bad angle.

5.8   Look for rhea farm.

6.7   Turn right at stop sign at T intersection onto Winnerline Road/TR 132.

7.5   Turn left at T intersection on OH–726.

7.6   Turn right to continue on Winnerline Road/TR 132.

8.4   Turn left at stop sign onto Monroe–Central Road.

9.3   Turn right onto Orphans Road/TR 127.

10.4   Turn left onto U.S. Highway 127. Road is busy; use caution.

10.6   Cross Interstate 70 bridge after passing Dairy Queen and Country Cooker on left. Ride carefully in area of on- and off-ramps for interstate.

11.1   Turn right onto Price Road.

13.4   Cross Geeting Bridge.

16.1   Turn left at Y intersection on Lewisburg–Western Road.

16.5   Turn right at Y intersection on Dayton Street in Lewisburg.

16.6   Cross Commerce Street/OH–503 at traffic signal.

16.8   Turn left to enter Lewisburg Community Park. The Dixon's Branch Covered Bridge is the park picnic shelter.

To leave park, go back down driveway.

17.0 Turn left at stop sign out of park onto what is now Salem Road.

17.5 Right at Y intersection onto Lewisburg Road.

18.1 Road becomes Lewisburg–Ozias Road/TR 418.

19.1 Turn right on New Market–Banta Road/TR 422. Enjoy the roller-coaster-type hills.

20.5 Turn right at stop sign onto Brennersville–Pyrmont Road/TR 453.

21.3 Cross OH–503. Use caution.

23.1 Road veers left and becomes Eaton–Lewisburg Road/TR 407.

27.9 Turn left onto Maple Street (before blue water tower).

29.4 Turn right at stop sign onto St. Clair Street.

29.4 End ride at William Bruce School on the left.

The Roberts Bridge, in Eaton only .2 mile into the ride, is the oldest of only six remaining double-barreled (two-lane) covered bridges in the United States. It was built in 1829 across Sevenmile Creek south of Eaton. In August 1986, an arsonist set fire to the bridge, destroying the roof and siding and scorching the supporting trusses. After four years of hard work by the Roberts Bridge Restoration Committee, the bridge was restored and enough money was raised to move it to its current site. Vehicle traffic is no longer allowed on the bridge.

The Christman (Mile 2.6), Geeting (Mile 13.4), and Dixon's Branch (Mile 16.8) bridges were three of fifteen bridges built in the county by Everett S. Sherman. Sherman was summoned to Preble County after a severe storm tore through the county in the early 1890s. The Christman Bridge was built in 1895, the

Geeting Bridge in 1894, and the Dixon's Branch Bridge in 1887.

The most unusual farm on this tour is the rhea farm at Mile 5.8. It's not a hallucination: You will see ostrichlike birds roaming the grounds.

The hilliest portion of this ride is a 1.5-mile stretch along New Market–Banta Road. These are the roller-coaster variety of hills that should allow you to build up enough momentum while going down to carry you up over the next hill.

DRINKS
ICE CREAM
POPCORN
SHAKES
Chippers & Dunn
YOGURT
SUNDAES
MALTS
GIFTS
KOOL COW
Bicycle Rental

Trailing Along the Little Miami

Number of miles:	26 (28 flat on rail–trail only)
Approximate pedaling time:	3 hours
Terrain:	Hills then flat
Traffic:	Busy around Loveland especially on weekends; many of the roads crossing the trail tend to be busy too
Surface:	Paved country roads and a sometimes narrow rail–trail
Things to see:	Towns of Loveland and Morrow, Little Miami National Scenic River and State Park
Facilities:	Plenty of food choices at the beginning and end (Loveland) and middle (Morrow) of the route; restrooms and water are also available in both towns

Southwestern Ohio is blessed with the Little Miami River. This beautiful peaceful river has long been a canoeist's delight, and it has been designated a national scenic river as well as an Ohio state park.

The Little Miami Scenic Trail also has been developing along the bed of the former Little Miami Railroad from Terrace Park, east of Cincinnati, northward, paralleling the river. The paved portion of the trail stretches 60 miles from Milford to Yellow Springs. (An extension north into Springfield is in the planning stages.) Almost all the trail is open to only non-motorized users: Bicyclists, hikers, skaters and equestrians, can enjoy the mostly wooded scenery without concern about passing cars and trucks.

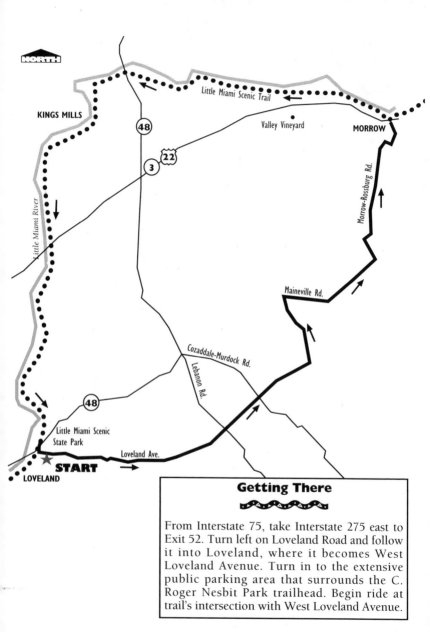

NORTH

KINGS MILLS

Little Miami Scenic Trail

Valley Vineyard

MORROW

48

3 22

Morrow-Rossburg Rd.

Little Miami River

Maineville Rd.

Cozaddale-Murdock Rd.

Lebanon Rd.

48

Little Miami Scenic
State Park

Loveland Ave.

★ START

LOVELAND

Getting There

From Interstate 75, take Interstate 275 east to
Exit 52. Turn left on Loveland Road and follow
it into Loveland, where it becomes West
Loveland Avenue. Turn in to the extensive
public parking area that surrounds the C.
Roger Nesbit Park trailhead. Begin ride at
trail's intersection with West Loveland Avenue.

DIREC-TIONS at a glance

0.0	Turn east onto West Loveland Avenue, which in 1 block becomes East Loveland Avenue. Go straight through traffic signal and start climbing out of town. After a while, the road's name changes to Dallasburg.
3.8	Continue straight across Murdock–Goshen Road at stop sign.
5.8	Turn left at stop sign onto Morrow–Cozaddale Road.
7.1	Turn right at stop sign onto Fosters–Maineville Road.
9.0	Turn left at stop sign at T intersection on Morrow–Rossburg Road.
9.4	Turn right at stop sign to remain on Morrow–Rossburg Road.
11.5	Turn left at stop sign onto Morrow–Woodville Road.
12.0	Continue straight at traffic signal, then turn left onto rail–trail.
26.0	Continue on path to return to start at West Loveland Avenue. There are many restaurants and snack shops along the trail before and after this intersection.

(Caution must be exercised at cross streets, however.)

As segments of the trail have been completed and more users have been attracted to it, the towns through which it passes have strived to become welcoming staging areas or wayside rests.

For instance in Loveland, myriad eateries, parking areas, and the wonderful C. Roger Nesbit Park have sprung up at trailside, offering places for tired, hungry or thirsty riders, skaters, and walkers to relax and restoke their furnaces. The Hawaiian Shave Ice stand opposite the Nesbit Park restrooms and amphitheater is particularly appealing on a hot summer day.

With 60 miles of trail, users can tailor trips lasting from several hours to several days to suit their own tastes. This ride, however, will include just a small portion of the trail and is focused on the wooded riverside. To enhance your appreciation of the landscape of the region, you'll begin the ride by climbing out of the river valley to ride through 10 miles of the surrounding rolling farmland. Your reward will be a nearly flat second half of the ride that passes through an almost unbroken tunnel of trees along the river. Of course, if you wish to flatten your tour, you can go out and back on the trail.

Morrow, 12 miles into the ride, has a trailside park with picnic and rest facilities, plus a few snack shops opposite the trail. If you want to make this a pedal-and-paddle excursion, there's a canoe livery several blocks from the trail on OH–123. The nearby Valley Vineyards Winery, located about 200 yards south of the trail on Stubbs Mill Road, offers daily tours and wine-tastings, too.

Here are a few considerations to keep in mind while on this ride: Auto traffic in and around Loveland and trail usage can be heavy, particularly on summer weekends. Exercise caution and courtesy to others, especially on the trail. Remember that many non-cyclists and novice cyclists are sharing the trail with you. Call out your intention to pass, slow down, or stop, and always be prepared to slow or even stop to avoid an accident. The speed limit on the trail is 20 m.p.h.

Ripley—Believe It or Ride

Number of miles:	15.8
Approximate pedaling time:	2 hours
Terrain:	Rolling to hilly
Surface:	Some very rough roads
Traffic:	Generally light except on state and federal routes
Things to see:	1875 North Pole Road Covered Bridge, Rankin House State Memorial; Ohio Tobacco, Ripley museums
Facilities:	Restaurants, stores, and bed-and-breakfast inns in Ripley; restaurant and bakery at Chief Logan's Gap Camp Resort

In this part of its course, the Ohio River cuts a deep cleft into the countryside. Ripley, a quaint small town, nestles on the strip of land between the mighty river and the hills that rise from the valley. This bike ride leaves Ripley the way its early residents would have: by paralleling one of the Ohio's tributaries and avoiding the steepest hills.

Although it would be impossible to avoid hills in this part of the Buckeye State, this ride is on quiet country roads over mostly rolling hills through pleasant woods and farmland. It would be a particularly beautiful fall ride.

Ripley was a stop on the Underground Railroad, the escape route taken by slaves from the South to freedom in Canada. High on Liberty Hill overlooking town stands the focal point of this activity, Rankin House. The Reverend John Rankin, a vocal aboli-

tionist preacher, opened his house regularly to fugitive slaves, hiding as many as twelve at a time. Rankin, his wife, and thirteen children were proud of never losing a "passenger" on the Underground Railroad. Today the house is open to the public as Rankin House State Memorial, where one can tour the house and climb a replica of the "stairway to liberty" that the fleeing slaves walked on. It is open noon to 5:00 P.M. Wednesdays through Sundays Memorial Day through Labor Day weekends; noon to 5:00 P.M. weekends during May, September, and October.

You may want to skip visiting the Rankin House by bike because of its extremely steep driveway. Tour the house before or after your bike ride, unless you have quadriceps of steel. The home is west of downtown. From U.S. Highway 68, turn right onto U.S. Highway 52/Second Street. Go through two traffic signals, then go right at the Y intersection where Highway 52 branches off. Immediately turn right and climb Rankin Hill Road to the memorial.

Ripley is also known as a collection point where tobacco growers from the surrounding area bring their crops. There are at least two tobacco warehouses in town, plus a tobacco museum where visitors can learn about tobacco farming. The museum is on U.S. Highway 52 near the start of the ride. It is open noon to 6:00 P.M. Mondays through Saturdays except in February and March.

After you climb out of the valley on Scoffield Road/Brown County 49, be sure to stop and look behind you for a pretty view of the Ohio River Valley when you crest the hill.

About 9.5 miles into your ride, be careful of the steep, twisting, and rough downhill stretch leading to the 1875 North Pole Road Covered Bridge. This bridge was seriously damaged in the flooding of spring 1997, but repairs were under way at the time this book was completed. You'll encounter another rough stretch at Mile 11.5.

If riding the hills leaves you hungry, consider stopping at Chief Logan's Gap Camp Resort, which has a restaurant and

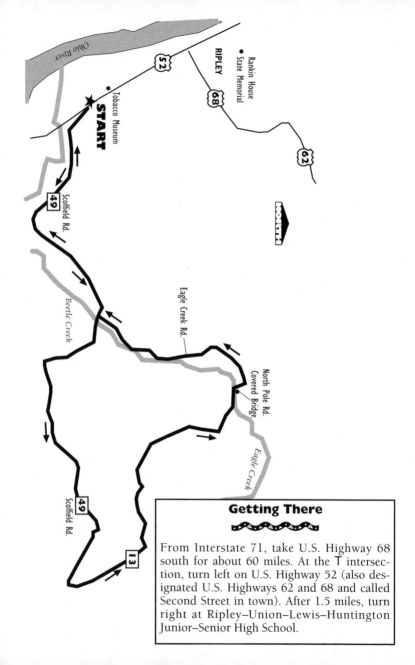

Ohio River

52

RIPLEY

• Rankin House
State Memorial

68

62

★ START
• Tobacco Museum

NORTH

49 Scoffield Rd.

Beetle Creek

Eagle Creek Rd.

North Pole Rd.
Covered Bridge

Eagle Creek

49 Scoffield Rd.

13

Getting There

From Interstate 71, take U.S. Highway 68 south for about 60 miles. At the T intersection, turn left on U.S. Highway 52 (also designated U.S. Highways 62 and 68 and called Second Street in town). After 1.5 miles, turn right at Ripley–Union–Lewis–Huntington Junior–Senior High School.

DIREC-TIONS at a glance

0.0	Turn right out of school parking lot at stop sign onto U.S. Highways 52/62/68.
0.1	Turn left onto Scoffield Road/Brown County 49 and start climbing.
3.8	Turn left at Y intersection to continue on Scoffield/CR 49.
6.7	Turn left onto North Pole Road/CR 13.
10.5	Cross North Pole Road Bridge.
10.9	Turn left onto unmarked Eagle Creek Road/Township Highway 28 paralleling Eagle Creek.
12.8	Turn right at stop sign at T intersection onto Scoffield Road/CR 49. Power plant smokestacks are visible straight ahead; graveyard is on right.
15.5	Turn right at stop sign at T intersection onto U.S. Highway 52/62/68.
15.7	Turn left at RULH Junior–Senior High School.
15.8	End ride in school parking lot.

bakery. From here it is about 1.5 miles back to your starting point, most of it downhill.

Also located just west of downtown is the Ripley Museum, at 219 North Second Street. The museum is an 1837 frame structure housing ten rooms filled with collectibles, some dating to the 1700s. It is open 1:30 to 5:00 P.M. Saturdays and Sundays (weekdays by appointment).

What's Wright with Dayton

Number of miles:	22.8
Approximate pedaling time:	3 hours
Terrain:	Hilly, flat, then hilly
Traffic:	Busy in some parts of this urban ride
Things to see:	Dayton Aviation Heritage National Historical Park and other Wright brothers historical sites, River Corridor Bikeway, Carillon Historical Park
Facilities:	Restrooms, water, and snacks at Carillon Park; restrooms, water, and picnic shelter at Island MetroPark; rest-rooms and water at Kettering Athletic Fields

On this ride, you never will be out of sight or hearing of the hustle and bustle of a major metropolitan area, but you will ride on surprisingly few major roads. Along the way, you'll learn a little about Dayton's most famous sons.

In December 1892, Orville and Wilbur Wright opened their first bicycle shop, The Wright Cycle Exchange. Business blossomed, and over the next fourteen years the brothers ran six different shops. In 1896 the brothers started dabbling in aviation. Using mechanical knowledge gained at their shops, they built aeronautical testing equipment and airplane components from common bike parts.

On December 17, 1903, the Wrights flew the first heavier-than-air machine at Kitty Hawk, North Carolina. They returned home

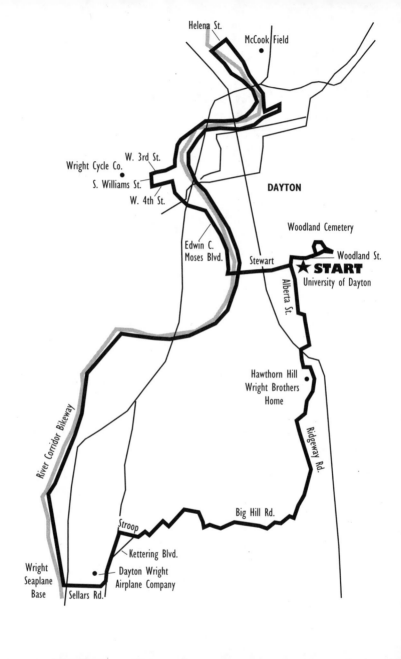

Helena St.

McCook Field

Wright Cycle Co.

W. 3rd St.

S. Williams St.

W. 4th St.

DAYTON

Woodland Cemetery

Edwin C.
Moses Blvd.

Stewart

Woodland St.

★ START

University of Dayton

Alberta St.

Hawthorn Hill
Wright Brothers
Home

Ridgeway Rd.

River Corridor Bikeway

Big Hill Rd.

Stroop

Kettering Blvd.

Wright
Seaplane
Base

Dayton Wright
Airplane Company

Sellars Rd.

DIREC-TIONS at a glance

0.0   Head down Woodland Avenue away from Woodland Cemetery.

0.1   Turn left at stop sign onto Alberta Street.

0.2   Cross Stewart Street at traffic signal to continue on Alberta Street.

0.3   Go right onto L Street at curve.

0.4   Turn left into Parking Lot P and cross through it to Caldwell Street; turn left out of the parking lot.

0.5   Turn right back onto Alberta Street.

0.8   Turn left at stop sign at T intersection onto Irving Avenue. Use caution: busy street.

0.8   Turn right onto Glendora Avenue.

1.2   Turn right at stop sign at T intersection onto Lookout Drive.

1.3   Turn right at stop sign at T intersection onto Thruston Boulevard.

1.4   Turn left, but not the sharpest left, at traffic signal to cross busy Far Hills Avenue/OH–48 and continue onto Oakwood Avenue. Use pedestrian signal and crosswalk on left side of Thruston if necessary; this is a long light.

1.6   Turn left at stop sign onto Dixon Avenue.

1.7   Turn right at traffic signal onto Harman Avenue.

1.8   Hawthorn Hill is on right.

1.9   Turn right at stop sign at Y intersection onto Ridgeway Road.

3.4   Turn right at Y intersection onto Sunny Crest Lane.

Getting There

From Interstate 75, take the Stewart Street exit in Dayton. Go east on Stewart Street until you see the main entrance to the University of Dayton on the right. Turn left (away from the university) at the traffic signal onto Alberta Street. Turn right at the first stop sign onto Woodland Avenue and park on the street outside Woodland Cemetery.

3.5 Turn right onto Locust Camp Road.

3.6 Turn left at stop sign onto Big Hill Road. Use caution: steep, curvy downhill with stop sign at bottom.

4.2 Cross busy Southern Boulevard at stop sign. Uphill climb is followed by steep descent.

5.0 Turn left onto Lodi Place.

5.1 Turn right onto Waterbury Drive.

5.3 Turn right at stop sign onto Hoyle Place.

5.5 Turn left onto Fulton Avenue.

5.7 Turn right at stop sign onto Ebert Road.

5.7 Turn left at stop sign onto very busy Kettering Boulevard.

5.8 Turn right onto Moraine Circle to visit Kettering-Moraine Museum. To leave museum, return to Kettering Boulevard and turn right.

5.9 Turn right at traffic signal onto busy Stroop Road.

6.2 Turn left at traffic signal onto Springboro Pike/OH 741. (*Caution:* busy; beware of parallel sewer grates.)

6.7 Turn right at traffic signal onto Sellars Road.

7.2 Take sidewalk on right of bridge across Great Miami River.

7.3 Go down bike stairs to River Corridor Bikeway. Continue north, keeping the river to left.

8.8 Turn left at T intersection, where bikeway continues on River Road.

9.3 Turn left where bikeway leaves River Road.

11.5 Cross River Road to enter Carillon Park. To leave park, return to bikeway and turn right.

12.4 Cross Stewart Street at traffic signal and turn left immediately onto sidewalk/bikeway to cross bridge over Great Miami River.

12.5 Turn right to remain on bikeway after crossing river.

12.9 Go down small ramp at left onto Edwin C. Moses Boulevard and continue north. Caution: Do not go down the levee to the riverside.

13.7 Turn left onto West Fourth Street.

14.2 Turn right at stop sign onto South Williams Street.

14.3 Wright Cycle Co. is on right.

14.4 Turn right at traffic signal onto West Third Street.

14.6 At traffic signal, cross Edwin C. Moses Boulevard, then immediately cross to other side of Third Street. Follow the sidewalk straight ahead—don't follow the bike path sign—through park to riverbank.

14.7 Turn left onto sidewalk paralleling river, then walk down bike stairs on right. At bottom of stairs, turn left and cross Wolf Creek to continue north.

16.9 Turn right on sidewalk at Helena Street to follow bikeway across bridge. *Caution:* Sidewalk is extremely narrow.

17.0 Island MetroPark is on left, across Helena Street.

17.1 Turn right to continue on bikeway.

17.3 Kettering Athletic Field is on left.

18.2 Turn right onto sidewalk and cross Webster Street Bridge over Mad River. Turn sharply right just after bridge to continue on bikeway.

21.1 Turn left onto Stewart Street at traffic signal.

21.4 Cross Main Street–OH 48 at traffic signal.

21.8 Turn left onto Alberta Street at traffic signal.

21.9 Turn right at stop sign onto Woodland Avenue to enter Woodland Cemetery.

22.0 Turn left (not sharpest left) at unmarked intersection. Woodhull monument is straight ahead.

22.2 Turn left at Y intersection and pass Lowes mausoleum on right.

22.3 Continue straight at crossroads past Thomas Staniland mausoleum on right.

22.3 At crossroads, a small flowerbed and sign on right mark the section where the Wrights are buried.

22.3 Backtrack a little from flowerbed, take first right and go uphill.

22.4 Turn right at Y intersection to continue around overlook.

22.5 Steps on left of road go up to downtown Dayton overlook. To leave, go right down steep hill.

22.7 Turn sharply left at hairpin turn at William Huffman memorial, turn right, and pass Woodland Cemetery Mausoleum on left.

22.8 Exit cemetery onto Woodland Avenue to end ride.

---

and perfected their technology and flying techniques in and around Dayton.

The brothers built their home, Hawthorn Hill, in Oakwood (Mile 1.8) after achieving fame and winning government contracts for their invention. Although Wilbur died in 1912, two years before the mansion's completion, Orville and his father lived here until their deaths in 1948 and 1917, respectively.

While the mansion is not open to the public, some of its furniture is on display at the Kettering-Moraine Museum (Mile 5.8). The museum, chronicling the history of Kettering and Moraine, is just off Kettering Boulevard near Stroop Road. It is open from 1:00 to 5:00 P.M. Sundays.

This ride goes through the massive General Motors truck-assembly plant in Moraine because part of this complex once was occupied by the Dayton Wright Airplane Company. The plant was razed in spring 1996; all that is left is a signpost on the road at Mile 6.4 indicating its former location.

Traffic can be heavy near the GM plant during the workweek. Also, be aware of the parallel sewer grates on Springboro Pike/OH–741.

When you reach the Great Miami River on the Sellars Road bridge, look below to see the site of the Wright Seaplane Base. From just south of the bridge and stretching north on the river, Orville Wright tested Wright Company seaplanes from 1911 to 1913.

Walk down the bike stairs from the bridge to the Horace M. Huffman Jr. River Corridor. This corridor, named after the former chief executive of local bicycle manufacturer Huffy

Corporation, stretches nearly 30 miles along the Great Miami River. You will glide on the River Corridor Bikeway through the heart of downtown Dayton, freeing you to enjoy the vista of the Dayton skyline as well as the natural beauty of the river.

Another Wright site along the River Corridor Bikeway is Carillon Historical Park, at Mile 11.5. This park has a replica of the Wright brothers' last bicycle shop and Wright Hall, housing the original Wright *Flyer III*, the world's first practical airplane. Also at the park are other items depicting the history of the Miami Valley. The park is open from May 1 to October 1, 10:00 A.M. to 8:00 P.M. Tuesdays through Saturdays and 1:00 to 8:00 P.M. Sundays.

At Mile 14.3 is the Wright Cycle Co. at 22 South Williams Street, where the Wright brothers first started developing the airplane. This building has been restored as part of the Dayton Aviation Heritage National Historical Park. It is open Memorial Day through Labor Day, 8:00 A.M. to 5:00 P.M. Mondays through Fridays, 10:00 A.M. to 4:00 P.M. Saturdays, and noon to 4:00 P.M. Sundays. It is open the rest of the year from 10:00 A.M. to 4:00 P.M. Saturdays, noon to 4:00 P.M. Sundays, and by appointment the rest of the week.

Returning to the bikeway, at Mile 17.3 you'll see the Kettering Athletic Field on your left. The athletic fields and the housing project behind them sit on the former site of McCook Field, the first U.S. military aviation research center. It was established in 1917, six months after the United States entered World War I. Among other things, the parachute was developed here.

It is fitting that the final two stops on this tour are truly high points. Orville and Wilbur Wright are buried with their parents and sister high on a hill in Woodland Cemetery, which is particularly beautiful in fall and spring. The unpretentious Wright family monument is about 50 yards off the road from a small flowerbed and sign. If you wish to end your ride with a spectacular overview of Dayton after visiting the Wright family plot, turn around and ride upward another couple tenths of a mile. Then, swoop down a steep, curvy hill to end your "flight" through a fraction of Dayton's aviation history.

 **Milling About Greene County**

Number of miles:	21.2 (25.2 for longer ride)
Approximate pedaling time:	2.5 (3 for longer ride) hours
Terrain:	Gently rolling with a few hills
Things to see:	Villages of Yellow Springs and Clifton, Clifton Mill, Clifton Gorge State Nature Preserve, Glen Helen, covered bridges, Grinnell Mill
Facilities:	Restaurants and stores (including a bike shop and bike-rental concession) in Yellow Springs, Clifton, and .3 mile off route at Young's Jersey Dairy; water and restrooms in Bryan Community Center; and picnic tables, restrooms, water, and camping at John Bryan State Park, just northeast of Yellow Springs

The allure of this ride is all in the name Greene County. Green it is, lush and full, and home to some of the best cycling in Ohio. This part of the county has a perfect mix of well paved, lightly traveled roads and terrain that is not too flat yet not too hilly. It has the largest working grist mill in the United States, an old abandoned mill, scenic Clifton Gorge, and some covered bridges. No wonder other Ohio counties are Greene with envy.

You'll begin and end your ride in the vibrant little village of Yellow Springs. The village is home to Antioch University, a wonderfully eclectic mix of shops and eateries, and a trailhead

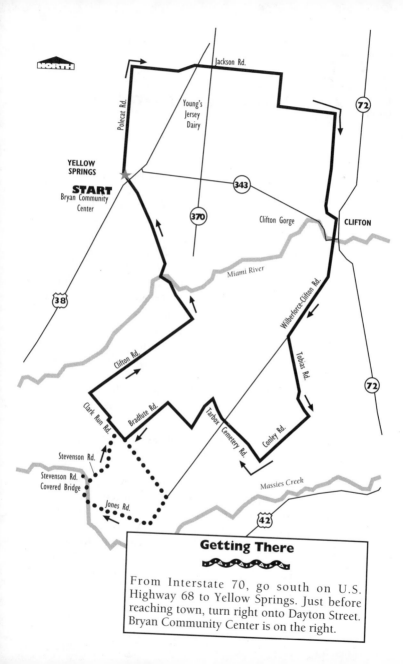

NORTH

Jackson Rd.

Polecat Rd.

Young's Jersey Dairy

72

YELLOW SPRINGS

START
Bryan Community Center

343

370

Clifton Gorge

CLIFTON

38

Miami River

Clifton Rd.

Wilberforce-Clifton Rd.

72

Clark Run Rd.

Bradfute Rd.

Tobias Rd.

Tarbox Cemetery Rd.

Conley Rd.

Stevenson Rd.

Stevenson Rd. Covered Bridge

Jones Rd.

Massies Creek

42

Getting There

From Interstate 70, go south on U.S. Highway 68 to Yellow Springs. Just before reaching town, turn right onto Dayton Street. Bryan Community Center is on the right.

DIREC-TIONS at a glance

0.0	Turn right on Dayton Street to leave Bryan Community Center.
0.1	Turn right onto Walnut Street.
0.4	Walnut Street becomes Polecat Road.
1.9	Turn right onto Jackson Road.

3.0 Cross U.S. Highway 68 at stop sign. (To visit Young's Jersey Dairy, turn right onto U.S. Highway 68 and ride .3 mile. Dairy is on left. To return to the route, turn right out of dairy onto U.S. Highway 68 and return to Jackson Road. Turn right. (The highway is busy but has a wide, paved shoulder.)

4.6 Go straight on Tanyard where Jackson turns left.

5.8 Turn left at stop sign at T intersection to continue on Tanyard.

7.4 Turn right onto Jackson Street.

7.7 Clifton Gorge State Nature Preserve is on right.

7.8 Road takes ninety-degree left turn and becomes Water Street.

7.9 Cross Clay Street at stop sign and enter driveway to Clifton Mill. To leave mill, turn left onto Water Street, then left onto Clay Street at the stop sign.

8.0 Clay becomes Wilberforce–Clifton Road.

9.6 Turn left onto Tobias Road.

11.0 Turn right at Y intersection on Conley Road, then immediately cross Cedarville–Yellow Springs Road at stop sign.

12.1 Turn right at stop sign at T intersection onto Tarbox Cemetery Road.

13.4 Turn left at stop sign at T intersection onto Wilberforce–Clifton Road.

14.0 Turn right onto Bradfute Road.

15.6 Turn right at stop sign at T intersection onto Clark Run Road, or skip to below for longer route option, which includes Stevenson Road Covered Bridge.

16.5 Turn right at stop sign at T intersection onto Clifton Road.

18.6 Turn left at yellow flasher onto Grinnell Road.

19.3 Cross the Little Miami River. Grinnell Mill is on right.

19.5 Cemetery Road Covered Bridge is on left off road in Glen Helen.

20.3 Turn right onto Little Miami Scenic Trail.

21.2 Turn right off path to enter Bryan Community Center parking lot to end ride.

Longer route option, which includes 1877 Stevenson Road Covered Bridge:

15.6 Turn left at stop sign at T intersection onto Clark Run Road..

16.8 Turn right at stop sign at T intersection onto Wilberforce–Clifton Road.

17.4 Turn right onto Jones Road.

18.6 Stevenson Road Covered Bridge is to left. Continue straight (don't cross bridge) onto Stevenson Road and pedal uphill.

19.8 Turn left at stop sign at T intersection onto Clark Run Road.

20.5 Turn right at stop sign at T intersection onto Clifton Road. **Pick up directions from Mile 18.6 on shorter ride.**

on the Little Miami Scenic Trail. The latter is a still-expanding multi-use path reserved for non-motorized travelers. Summer weekends see crowds of shoppers, cyclists, and skaters thronging the village.

Also in Yellow Springs is Glen Helen, an outdoor-education center owned by Antioch University. Hiking trails crisscrossing the nearly 1,000-acre preserve will bring you to the spring that gave the village its name and the remnants of what was once a thriving health and vacation resort. A small museum and entry to a number of hiking paths are just off the Little Miami Scenic Trail as you head into town at the end of the ride.

Another reason to bring your hiking shoes along on this ride is the beautiful Clifton Gorge State Nature Preserve, which is accessible at Mile 7.7. The gorge is the result of erosion by a large meltwater river that originated in the receding Wisconsin Glacier centuries ago. The Little Miami River now rushes through the chasm. It does little to deepen its path, although it lends a medley of background sounds to any walk along the rim or through the gorge. Part of the gorge is in John Bryan State Park, offering easy access if you're camping there.

The sleepy quaint little village of Clifton is home to the six-story Clifton Mill, perched atop a 50-foot waterfall on the Little Miami. This mill, built in 1802, provided corn meal and flour to federal troops in the Civil War. Various flours and pancake mixes are still milled here. Visitors are welcome to take a self-guided tour of the grain-milling operation (fee charged), buy homemade pancake mixes and flour or other items in the gift shop, or dine in The Millrace Restaurant. Be sure to cross the river for the most scenic view of the mill and waterfall.

Grinnell Road offers looks at Grinnell Mill and the 1886 Cemetery Road Covered Bridge. The mill, no longer in operation, is at Mile 19.3 (23.3 on the longer option), and the bridge is .2 mile farther and about 50 feet off the road down a short path. Both are owned by Antioch University and are in peaceful settings should you need a breather.

If you would like to challenge yourself with slightly hillier terrain and visit a covered bridge built in 1877, take the slightly longer route option at the 15.6-mile mark.

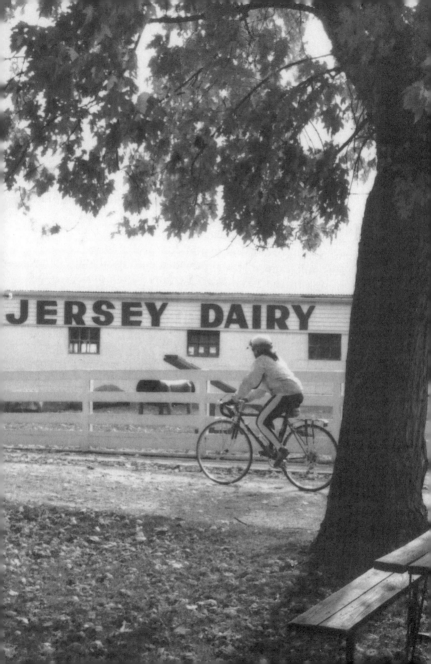

XYZ Ride

Number of miles:	23 (19.8 without side trip to Young's Jersey Dairy)
Approximate pedaling time:	2.5 hours
Terrain:	Nearly flat
Traffic:	No auto traffic except on U.S. Highway 68, where traffic tends to be heavy on weekends
Things to see:	Little Miami Scenic Trail, Little Miami River, Glen Helen Nature Preserve, Young's Jersey Dairy, Xenia, and Yellow Springs
Facilities:	Restaurants, stores, and bike shops in Xenia and Yellow Springs; bicycle/skate rentals in Yellow Springs; water, restrooms, and picnic tables at Old Town Reserve; water and restrooms in Bryan Community Center in Yellow Springs; camping at John Bryan State Park northeast of Yellow Springs

Here is an end-of-the-alphabet, out-and-back sampler of bicyclists' delights in Greene and Clark counties.

X is for Xenia. In 1846 Xenia was the hub for the Little Miami Railroad Company, which connected Cincinnati with Sandusky. Today this city of 25,000 is seeking to become a hub for bicyclists. Since October 1991, thousands of cyclists, in-line skaters, pedestrians, and equestrians have used the portion of

203

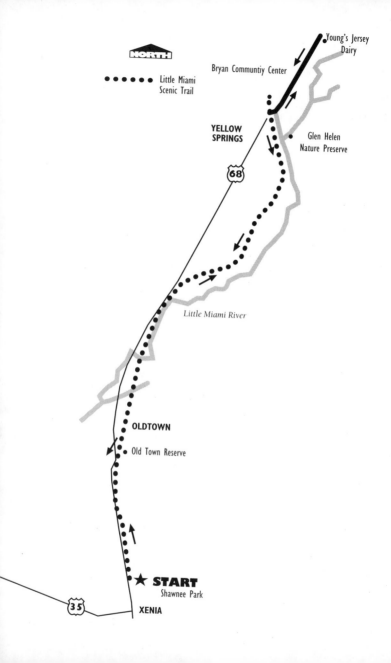

NORTH

●●●●●● Little Miami
Scenic Trail

Young's Jersey
Dairy

Bryan Communtiy Center

YELLOW
SPRINGS

Glen Helen
Nature Preserve

68

Little Miami River

OLDTOWN

Old Town Reserve

START
Shawnee Park

35

XENIA

DIREC-TIONS at a glance

0.0   From Shawnee Park, head north (right) on Little Miami Scenic Trail.

2.3   Old Town Reserve is on right.

9.2   Glen Helen Nature Preserve is on right.

9.9   Bryan Community Center is on the right, just a short way down Dayton Street.

To continue to Young's Jersey Dairy, turn left out of Bryan Center parking lot onto Dayton Street, then left again onto U.S. Highway 68. (*Caution: busy intersection.*) If you don't wish to go to Young's, turn around and return to Xenia on Little Miami Scenic Trail.

11.5   Turn right into Young's Jersey Dairy. To leave, turn left out of Young's parking lot onto U.S. Highway 68. (*Caution: busy road.*)

13.1   Turn left onto Little Miami Scenic Trail, at the first cross walk after the community center turn. (Again, use caution; traffic can be heavy.)

23.0   Turn left at Shawnee Park to end ride.

Getting There

While this ride is described with both its start and finish at Shawnee Park in Xenia, it can just as easily be started at the Bryan Community Center in Yellow Springs, or even at Young's Jersey Dairy. Parking, water, and restrooms are available at all three.

To Shawnee Park, Xenia: From Interstate 675, go east on U.S. Highway 35, then continue on U.S. Business Route 35. Turn left on North Detroit Street/U.S. Highway 68 at the Greene County Courthouse. After .1 mile, cross Church Street, veering slightly right onto Shawnee Parkway. Follow this street into the park.

To Bryan Community Center, Yellow Springs: From Interstate 70, go south on U.S. Highway 68 to Yellow Springs. Just before reaching town, turn right onto Dayton Street. Bryan Community Center is on the right.

To Young's Jersey Dairy: From Interstate 70, go south on U.S. Highway 68. Young's is on the left about 6 miles south of the interstate. Park in one of the outer parking lots as a courtesy to regular customers.

the Little Miami Scenic Trail stretching from Xenia about 10 miles to Yellow Springs. In 1997 a short segment of the path in Xenia was completed, linking this portion of the path with the 50-mile paved stretch of trail to Milford, east of Cincinnati.

Also in the works in 1997 was a seven-acre complex featuring a replica of Xenia Station, a former Pennsylvania Railroad hotel/depot, which is slated to house concessions, restrooms, and auto and bicycle parking for trail users. Xenia Station is to be the eventual meeting point of the Little Miami Scenic Trail, the Xenia–Jamestown Connector, the H-Connector (eventually linking Xenia and Dayton), and the Ohio to Erie Trail.

Old Town Reserve is about 2.3 miles north of your starting point in Shawnee Park. The great Shawnee Indian leader Tecumseh was born on the banks of a large spring here in 1768 while his parents were traveling from their home village on the Scioto River to a major tribal council at the Shawnee tribal capital of Chalahgawtha, located "two arrow flights" northwest of this site in present-day Oldtown.

Y is for Yellow Springs. On the other end of this stretch of the Little Miami Scenic Trail, the village of Yellow Springs is home to an eclectic mix of shops and Antioch University. Yellow Springs is an extremely popular weekend destination for people who want to shop and soak up the atmosphere, as well as for users of the rail–trail. This ride, therefore, is best done during the week. If you must ride on the weekend, try early in the morning or early in the evening. Area cyclists and skaters also enjoy using the trail after dark on summer nights (with appropriate lights on their bodies and bikes).

At Mile 9.4 of your ride is Glen Helen Nature Preserve run by Antioch University. There are hiking trails along which are the yellow spring the village is named after, and some old-growth virgin forest. There is also a small museum just off the trail.

Although there are a number of places to eat on or near the trail in Xenia and Yellow Springs, try to hold off for just a short while longer, because . . .

206

Z is for the "zoo" of farm animals at Young's Jersey Dairy. Young's, northeast of Yellow Springs on U.S. Highway 68, is famous in the greater Dayton area for its wonderful homemade ice cream. It is, consequently, packed day and night. In addition to the justifiably famous ice cream, Young's serves delicious sandwiches, soups, and baked goods. Patrons are welcome to visit the barn and pet and feed the livestock. There is also Udders 'N' Putters miniature golf next door.

The most direct way to Young's from Yellow Springs is north on U.S. Highway 68. Although the road can be busy, especially on weekends, its broad shoulder is more than adequate for safe cycling. The ride is slightly uphill all the way, but it's only 1.6 miles one way.

For More Information

Alum Creek State Park
3615 South Old State Road
Delaware, OH 43015
(614) 548–5409

Ashtabula County Covered
Bridge Festival
County Courthouse
25 West Jefferson Street
Jefferson, OH 44047
(216) 576–3769

Bicycle Museum of America
7 West Monroe Street
New Bremen, OH 45869
(419) 629–9249

Buccia Vineyard
518 Gore Road
Conneaut, OH 44030
(216) 593–5976
Open daily except Sundays.
B&B open seven days a week
year-round.

Campus Martius Museum
Ohio Historical Society
601 Second Street
Marietta, OH 45750
(800) 860–0145 or
(614) 373–3750

Open March through
November. Admission charged.

Cantwell's Old Mill Winery
403 South Broadway
Geneva, OH 44041
(216) 466–5560

Carillon Historical Park
2001 South Patterson
Boulevard
Dayton, OH 45409
(937) 293–2841
Open May 1 to October 1.
Admission charged.

Clermont County Convention
and Visitors' Bureau
4440 Glen Este–Withamsville
Road; Suite K
Cincinnati, OH 45245
(800) 796–4282 or
(513) 753–7211

Cleveland's Emerald Necklace
Cleveland MetroParks
4101 Fulton Parkway
Cleveland, OH 44144–1923
(216) 351–6300
Emerald Necklace map
available.

Columbus Zoo
P.O. Box 400
Powell, OH 43065–0400
(614) 645–3400
Open year-round. Admission
charged.

Covered Bridge Tour
Dayton Cycling Club
P.O. Box 94
Wright Brothers Station
Dayton, OH 45409–0094
Spring tours of 23, 45, 74, or
103 miles, covering two, five,
seven, or ten covered bridges,
respectively; participant fee.

Cuyahoga Valley Scenic
Railway "Bike and Hike"
excursions
P.O. Box 158
Peninsula, OH 442645–0158
(800) 468–4070
http://members.aol.com/cvsrail
Operates on a varied schedule
from early February through
December.

Dayton Aviation Heritage
National Historical Park
P.O. Box 9280
Wright Brothers Station
Dayton, OH 45409
(937) 225–7705

Open daily Memorial Day
through Labor Day, and on
weekends and by appointment
during the rest of the year.

Edison Birthplace Museum
4 Edison Drive
P.O. Box 451
Milan, OH 44846
(419) 499–2135
Guided tours offered January
through November. Admission
charged.

Ferrante Winery & Ristorante
5585 State Route 307
Geneva, OH 44041
(216) 466–VINO

Firelands Museum
Firelands Historical Society
4 Case Avenue
P.O. Box 572
Norwalk, OH 44857
(419) 668–6038
Open April through
November; admission charged.
Free guide to Norwalk's his-
toric houses is available.

German Village Society
588 South Third Street
Columbus, OH 43215
(614) 221–8888

Historic Clifton Mill and
Millrace Restaurant
75 Water Street
Clifton, OH 45316
(937) 767–5501
Open year-round. Admission
charged for mill.

Historic Roscoe Village
381 Hill Street
Coshocton, OH 43812
(800) 877–1830

Hocking Valley Scenic Railway
P.O. Box 427
Nelsonville, OH 45764
(614) 470–1300 weekdays or
(614) 753–9531 weekends
June through October. Trips offered on weekends, Memorial
Day through October; fares
vary.

Indian Mill State Memorial
Ohio Historical Society
1982 Velma Avenue
Columbus, OH 43211–2497
(419) 294–4022 or
in Ohio (800) 686–1545
Open Fridays, Saturdays, and
Sundays from Memorial Day
weekend through October;
admission charged.

Island Hopper Ferry
Drawbridge Boat Lines
North Jefferson Street
Port Clinton, OH 43452
(800) 90–FERRY

Isaac Ludwig Mill
Miami & Erie Canal
Providence Metropark
U.S. 24 at S.R. 578
Grand Rapids, OH 43522
(419) 832–6004
Open Wednesdays through
Fridays, weekends, and
holidays May through
October. Fee charged for
canal boat rides; mill admission is free. Craft demonstrations of blacksmithing,
coopering, and tinsmithing
are also given.

Jet Express ferry
North Jefferson Street
Port Clinton, OH 43452
(800) 245–1538
http://www.jet-express.com

Kelleys Island Chamber of
Commerce
P.O. Box 783M
Kelleys Island, OH 3438–0783
(419) 746–2360

Kettering–Moraine Museum
35 Moraine Circle South
Kettering, OH 45439
(937) 299–2722
Open from 1:00 to 5:00 P.M.
Sunday; admission charged.

Little Miami Scenic Trail
Warren County Convention
and Visitors Bureau
1073 Oregonia Road Suite A
Lebanon, OH 45036
(800) 617–OHIO or
(513) 932–1132

Malabar Farm State Park
4050 Bromfield Road
Lucas, OH 44843
(419) 892–2784
Open year-round. Fee charged
for guided tours of mansion.

Marblehead Lighthouse
Ohio Department of Natural
Resources
Division of Parks and
Recreation
East Harbor State Park
1169 North Buck Road
Lakeside-Marblehead, OH
43440–9610
(419) 734–4424

Milan Historical Museum, Inc.
10 Edison Drive,
P.O. Box 308
Milan, OH 44846
(419) 499–2968
Open April through October.
Donation requested.

Monticello III
Coshocton Park District
23253 State Route 83
Coshocton, OH 43812
(614) 622–7528
Canal boat tours offered daily
from Memorial Day through
Labor Day and on weekends
from Labor Day to mid-
October. Fee charged after
October.

Muskingum River Parkway
Muskingum River State Park
P.O. Box 2806
Zanesville, OH 43702–2806
(614) 452–3820 or
(614) 452–3147

Ohio & Erie Canal Towpath Trail
c/o Cuyahoga Valley National
Recreational Area
15610 Vaughn Road
Brecksville, OH 44141
(800) 445–9667 or
(216) 524–1497

Ohio Caverns
2210 State Route 245 East
West Liberty, OH 43357
(937) 465–4017
Open year-round except
Thanksgiving and Christmas
days. Admission charged.

Ohio Central Railroad
P.O. Box 427
111 Factory Street
Sugarcreek, OH 44681
(330) 852–4676

Ohio River Museum
Ohio Historical Society
Front and St. Clair Streets
Marietta, OH 45750
(800) 860–0145 or
(614) 373–3750
Open March through
November. Admission charged.

Ohio Tobacco Museum
P.O. Box 61
Ripley, OH 45167
(513) 392–4684
Open Monday through
Saturday April through
January. Admission charged.

Old Firehouse Winery
5499 Lake Road
P.O. Box 310
Geneva-on-the-Lake, OH 44041
(800) UNCORK–1 or
(216) 466–9300

Olentangy Indian Caverns
1779 Home Road
Delaware, OH 43015
(614) 548–7917
Open April through October.
Admission charged.

Piatt Castles
P.O. Box 507
West Liberty, OH 43357
(937) 465–2821
Open March through October.
Admission charged.

Rankin House State Memorial
Ripley Heritage Inc./
Ohio Historical Society
P.O. Box 176
Ripley, OH 45167
(513) 392–1627
(513) 392–4660, or
(513) 392–4377
Open May through October.
Admission charged.

Ripley Museum
Ripley Heritage Inc.
P.O. Box 176
Ripley, OH 45167
(513) 392–1627,
(513) 392–4660, or
(513) 392–4377
Open weekends and by appointment only on weekdays. Admission charged.

Robbins' Crossing
Hocking College
3301 Hocking Parkway
Nelsonville, OH 45764–9704
(614) 753–3591
Historic skills demonstrations. Free.

Sauder Farm and Craft Village
State Route 2
P.O. Box 235
Archbold, OH 43502
(800) 590–9755
e-mail:
102671.3365@compuserve.com
Open mid-April through late October. Admission charged. Restaurant, bakery, and inn are open year-round; a campground is open in summer.

South Bass Island
Put-in-Bay Chamber of Commerce
P.O. Box 250
Harbour Square
Put-in-Bay, OH 43456
(419) 285–2832

Steubenville City of Murals
P.O. Box 428
Steubenville, OH 43952
(614) 282–0938 Tuesdays through Fridays

TOSRV—Tour of the Scioto River Valley
Columbus Outdoor Pursuits
P.O. Box 14384
Columbus, OH 43214–0384
(614) 447–1006
e-mail:
76774.631@compuserve.com
Send a self-addressed, stamped envelope with queries by mail.

Wyandot Lake
10101 Riverside Drive
Powell, OH 43065
(800) 328–9283 or
(614) 889–9283
Amusement and water park, open summers only. Admission charged.

Bibliographic Resources

General facts about Ohio
Benson, Margorie. *Awesome Almanac: Ohio*. Walworth, Wis.: B&B Publications, 1995.
Traylor, Jeff. *Ohio Pride: A Guide to Ohio Roadside History*. Columbus, Ohio: Backroad Chronicles, 1990.
Vonada, Damaine, ed. *The Ohio Almanac*. Wilmington, Ohio: Orange Frazer Press, 1992.

American Indian history
Vogel, John J. *Indians of Ohio and Wyandot County*. New York: Vantage Press, 1975.

The Amish
Good, Merle and Phyllis. *20 Most Asked Questions about the Amish and Mennonites*. Intercourse, Pa.: Good Books, 1995.
Hostetler, John. *Amish Life*. Scottsdale, Pa.: Herald Press, 1983.

Canals
Gieck, Jack. *A Photo Album of Ohio's Canal Era, 1825–1913*. Kent, Ohio: Kent State University Press, 1992.

Covered bridges
Wood, Miriam. *The Covered Bridges of Ohio: An Atlas and History*. Columbus, Ohio: Old Trail Printing Company, 1993.

Dayton's aviation history
Johnson, Mary Ann. *A Field Guide to Flight: On the Aviation Trail in Dayton, Ohio*. Dayton, Ohio: Landfall Press, 1986.

Glen Helen
Leuba, Clarence. *Guide to Historical Spots in Glen Helen*. Yellow Springs, Ohio: Antioch Bookplate Company, 1978.

State parks
Weber, Art. *Ohio State Parks: A Guide to Ohio's State Parks.* Clarkston, Mich.: Glovebox Guidebook Publications, 1993.

Acknowledgments

This book would not have been possible without the help of many relatives, friends, and acquaintances, both in and out of Ohio.

First and foremost, I thank my husband, Mark, whose many suggestions were invaluable. His patience and enthusiasm through many miles of travel were also inspiring. I look forward to exploring these many sites with him at a much more leisurely pace!

Thanks to my good friend Janet Long, who always had an encouraging word and was always willing to explore another region of Ohio or proofread a ride.

Thanks as well to other friends and relatives who accompanied me during my travels: Mary, Mark, Diane and Laura Buchwalder; Josh Findley; Alex Van Atta; and Jack and Rebecca Minardi.

Thanks to my colleagues at the *Dayton Daily News* who helped free me at critical times to complete this project, especially my supervisor, Hap Cawood.

Thanks to my brother Rick Wert for critiquing my writing.

My thanks also go to those who—knowingly or unknowingly—offered ideas for rides, including members of the Ohio Bicycling Federation and the Dayton Cycling Club; Tom Barlow and other Columbus Outdoor Pursuits members who plan the annual Great Ohio Bicycle Adventure and the Tour of the Scioto River Valley; Allan Chester of the Heart of Ohio Tailwinds Bicycle Club, Marion; Dale E. Foltz of the Seneca Sprockets Bicycle Club, Tiffin; Claire Lea of the Dayton Cycling Club; Chuck Smith of the Dayton Cycling Club and Ohio Bicycling Federation; and Hillary Sullivan of the Akron Bicycle Club.

Thanks as well to the following, who offered detailed information about routes and/or interesting sites on specific rides included in this book:

Flat Farm Frolic: James H. Roth, moderator of the Tailwind Bicycle Club at St. Francis de Sales High School, Toledo

Wood County Wander: James H. Roth

Blazing Through the Firelands: Peggy and Jim Lonz of Norwalk

Emerald Necklace: Matt Tomacheski and Sue Webster of the Cleveland area

Cross-State Challenge: Richard King of Old Fort Steuben Project, Inc., Steubenville

Cinnamon Bun Delight: Mary and Mark Buchwalder of the Dayton Cycling Club

Ohio's Interstate 1: Dick Seebode of the Ohio Bicycle Federation

A Scoop of Licking County: Mary Buchwalder and Janet Long of the Dayton Cycling Club

Seal of Approval Ride: Delbert Doles of the Dayton Cycling Club

Lose Your Head in Marietta: Mark Buchwalder

Biketoberfest: Annette Thompson of the Bicycle Museum of America, and Dee Littlejohn of Crown Equipment Corp., New Bremen

Bridges of Preble County: Mary and Mark Buchwalder

Trailing Along the Little Miami: Donna Boutilier of the Cincinnati Cycle Club

Milling About Greene County: Steve Buchwalder of the Dayton Cycling Club

Thanks to those who offered a place to stay during my travels: Peggy and Jim Lonz, Sue and Mike Webster.

Thanks to Mary Ann and Jeff Van Atta for the use of their office equipment.

Thanks to photo models Mark Minardi, Mary and Mark Buchwalder, Claire Lea, Alex Van Atta, and Cathy and Elizabeth Wirrig.

Last but not least, thanks to everyone who offered moral support during this project. These include, but are not limited to, Mark Minardi, Clara, Rick and Tina Wert, the entire Minardi family, Mary and Mark Buchwalder, Janet Long, Linda and Mike Crider, and Roz Young.

About the Author

Kay Wert Minardi has been an avid cyclist since 1982. Her hobby became a passion in 1987 when she rode across the United States with a BikeCentennial group. Today, as editorial page copy editor for the *Dayton Daily News*, she commutes to work on her bike. She is president of the Dayton Cycling Club, a 1,000-member not-for-profit educational and recreational organization for bicycle touring and racing in the Miami Valley, and she writes a monthly column and occasional articles for *Spoke 'N' Link*, the Dayton Cycling Club's newsletter. Kay cycles around Ohio on weekends, and every year she takes family members on the one-week Great Ohio Bicycle Adventure.